Top
T.

SON OF LONDON

SON OF LONDON

by

THOMAS BURKE

HERBERT JENKINS LIMITED
3 DUKE OF YORK STREET, ST. JAMES'S
LONDON, S.W.I

To

A LONDON SUBURB

with the author's love

THIS BOOK IS PRODUCED
IN COMPLETE CONFORMITY WITH
THE AUTHORISED ECONOMY STANDARDS

Printed in Great Britain by Butler & Tanner Ltd., Frome and London

CONTENTS

CHAP.		PAGE
I.	SEEING LIFE	7
II.	BOY AND GIRL	12
III.	OLD-TIME SUBURB	37
IV.	MAGIC AND MUSIC	56
V.	SWEET LAVENDER	71
VI.	FLYING ANGEL	87
VII.	GOOD-BYE FOR EVER	107
VIII.	GROWING PAINS	121
IX.	FREE LANCE	156
X.	OCCASIONS AND ENCOUNTERS	186

SON OF LONDON

CHAPTER I

SEEING LIFE

THEY were asking £25 for it, that Bond Street gallery, and I thought the price was reasonable. It was a Kate Greenaway water-colour, and it showed a farm-house with a paddock on one side, and on the other a sloping meadow ; and in the meadow was a group of angelic children, in pinafores white and clean beyond nature, picking angelic flowers. As art it may have been this or that ; one does not apply arbitrary measures to K. G. As a key to a long-locked door it was, to me, well worth its price. I had seen that picture many years earlier, reproduced in one of her *Almanacks*. It was the first of this world's pictures I remember seeing. I had never seen it since.

I decided to have it. But in the few moments between entering the gallery and waiting for the assistant, the key began to turn, and the old door opened, and out rushed across the heart's eye a cloud of tiny memories, motes in a beam from a Magic Lantern, dusty but golden, and I was caught up in the bliss of remembered bliss. I recalled the occasion of my first seeing that picture, and away went the accumulated years, and I was out of Bond Street and out of that day and these thrilling hours, and back in the complacent jog-trot tempo of the opening 'nineties.

. . . . .

I was five years old, and I was in a small candle-lit room in a small house in a dim by-street of a South London suburb, standing as it were in a vortex whirling with the hues of glory. The glory was composed of many elements ; of the street whose rumour came faintly through closed curtains ; of a bright wood fire ; of sprigs of green stuff with scarlet berries ; of Kate Greenaway's pictures, and the odour of tangerine oranges and the frosty glitter of mince-pies, and a coloured catalogue of Dickins & Jones ; of the unearthly mystery of voices in the outer dark singing songs about Good Kings and Shepherds ; of shops radiant with storms of light and unimagined treasure ; of cards showing scenes in crimson and green and gold of baronial halls or village streets or cottages with lit windows in landscapes of snow, into all of which I could enter as into the rooms of a real house or into the street round the corner ; and of the carnival shapes of tins and boxes, and the gay trifles called crackers.

At the heart of this glory was something that was called Christmas, and this Christmas illuminated the people about me, and my feelings and sensations, as it illuminated the room. It was not a date in a calendar, a day of the year, a celebration or a holiday. It was a living presence that set the air tingling, and pervaded all things and transfigured them with its burst of colour—colour blushing, blazing, shining, sparkling. It had brought at once a hush and a stir ; a hush of common living and a stir of new and vital being. For the first time in my short memory life had come alive ; everybody had woken up ; and in that exaltation they all, even the most tiresome, became dear to me, and all things became charged with goodness. That, I felt, was Real Life. All I had known before in my five years, all I had heard talked of as Real Life, had been a grey sham. That something called Christmas was life as I remembered it at some time that I couldn't really remember ; some time before I entered the cage of this world and that dim street and that little room. Everything was resolved into living colour and odour and delight— the bright eyes of crystallised fruits, the odour of burning wood, the glow of oranges and the purple of the wet streets, and the miles of grieving lamplight

whose very grievousness was delight—all were fused
into one harmony of spirit and sense called Christmas.

The miracle had been wrought of simple things.
There was seldom, in that home, a sixpence to spare
at the week's end, but out of a handful of hoarded
coppers an effect was created of the bursting of a
flower into bloom. A few penny toys ; a few halfpenny Christmas-cards ; a ha'porth of holly ; a four-
penny box of crackers ; a sixpenny box of crystallised
fruits ; a present of mince-pies ; a more generous fire
than usual, and two candles instead of one, and somebody's discarded Kate Greenaway book—and up came
that mystery, or sense of mystery, which is the true
Christmas.

And that celestial adventure, the pantomime. . . .
That, too, I felt, was Real Life. It was real and right
that people were fleet-footed gods and goddesses,
glistening in white and silver and green, and using
the speech of song ; and it was wrong for them to
shuffle about in ugly clothes and look like sinners. It
was real and right that toil was squalid and that
idleness was blessed. It was real and right that rooms
should be lakes of lustre, and that roads should disappear through depths of light into the everlasting
hills. It was real and right that policemen should be
prodded with red-hot pokers, that strings of sausages
should be found where they are wanted, and that
silly old interfering pantaloons should be tripped up.
It was real and right that we should win our heart's
desire, and that valiant souls should be invulnerable
before the baseness of greed and power. The thing
called Christmas had broken down the wall that people
built between themselves and Real Life, and was
showing life as itself. And nobody around me seemed
to see it. They seemed to think it was a holiday from
reality, an amusing make-believe. But I was sure I
was seeing truth.

And once again, before I was six, I saw. Again, in
the succeeding spring, I encountered Real Life. I

was at a large house with garden, orchard, meadow, stables. I forget how I came to be there, but I had slept the night there, and had had all the excitement which a night in a different house always gives to a child. There was the different bedroom with a different smell to it, a different wall-paper on which one could trace new faces and new forms, different pictures and ornaments—all of them not only different but wearing also a strangeness. There were different shadows in the corners, a different note in the tick of the clock, and something very different and significant, but uncommunicative, in the shape of the chairs. Those things had a life among other people of which I knew nothing, and they were not going to let the stranger know what they knew.

As soon as it was light, I was up, and after breakfast in the kitchen, with the fresh excitement of different table, different crockery, and a different taste to the bread, I had gone into the garden. They had told me it was Springtime. The word was new to me, to be stored away for consideration ; yet at the same time it was familiar. Springtime . . . and then I was lying on the grass at the back of the white house with my head in a clump of daffodils and my eyes exploring the country of gold inside the trumpet of one of its blossoms.

It was a morning that seemed as though it were the first morning of the world ; a morning in a high key with a clean sky and brilliant sun ; and the white house, standing among the sparkling grass, shone back at the sun. At one side of it was a bank of what I was told were white violets, and above the bank was what was called hawthorn. On the other side was a bank of primrose, and behind that was the pink and white of the orchard. All around me was gold and white and green, and above me was a singing blue. The still scene was as lively as a dance, and yet so quiet that in my already excited state I had the fancy that I could almost hear the passing of time.

Every blossom was throwing to the air its separate
perfume, and with the keen sense of childhood I could
catch singly the perfume of earth and grass and
daffodil, of apple and primrose and hawthorn, and
they crowded into my heart, where they lie to this
day. And all those perfumes, and the colour and the
dew and the skylarks, seemed, to my excited nerves,
to fuse and make one presence which was Morning ;
and the Morning seemed like another child asking me
to play with it. There was a spirit about the grass
and the flowers and the trees which suggested that
Morning had woken up as excited as myself, because it
was to be a great day, and was now romping about,
not in abandon but with an air of being in the secret
of some delightful impending climax.

It was my first sight of a real garden, and I saw its
hundred details not only with my eyes but with my
whole being. I absorbed it through every sense and
every perception. Just as the new word Springtime
seemed familiar, so on those banks alight with the
almost-speaking faces of little flowers, I had a feeling
of coming back to something I had always known ;
of resuming a life in which streets and shops had been
only an interlude. The Morning seemed so close to
me that I was not only in the garden ; I was inside
that Morning, and I lay staring into the daffodil until
I was part of a Morning in which I breathed gold
perfume and drank gold air and heard gold sounds.

There was no climax. The Morning moved on to
noon by paces as secret and as certain as the paces of
the hour-hand of the clock, and the trees stilled themselves and stood in the immobility of meditation, and
the grass ceased to sparkle, and the Morning passed
and made way for a new and graver presence called
Afternoon. But it had made itself known to me. I
had seen the life of Life. All the rest was imitation.
The Real Life my elders spoke of was, according to
them, something cold and stark and grim, something
that was always trying to catch you when you weren't

looking, and trip you up.   But that Morning confirmed
that Christmas, and told me they were wrong.   Real
Life was in that singing blue and in the trumpets and
shells and bells of those flowers.

It seemed to me then, as it had seemed at Christmas,
that being grown up meant being half-asleep.   I
couldn't understand how they could go about as they
did, looking so glum, making life so heavy and dour.
Without knowing it, I had stumbled on the truth
that in the imagination, which common sense fears
and distrusts, is the only genuine life, the life of Life,
which is the food of the spirit and which no material
circumstance or outer turmoil can ever trespass upon
or spoil.

In talking to adults and to most other boys and
girls I was often aware of obstacles.   They were all
so what was called sensible, so concerned with what
were called Facts.   They were always saying What-
do-you-mean ? or How-do-you-make-that-out ? or I-
can't-understand-half-you-say.   I was always getting
annoyed with them for not understanding, or annoyed
with myself for not being like them.   I wasn't sure
what Facts were, but I couldn't share their veneration
for them.   I knew that life was more full of delight
than they said it was, and I could not understand
why they could not feel and live on the pitch of that
Christmas or that Morning.   Not until I was ten did
I meet one who could.

CHAPTER II

BOY AND GIRL

AS I stood in that Bond Street gallery, gazing at
that Greenaway picture, I recalled a passage
in Spielmann's book about her.

Kate Greenaway, the Londoner of the rustic name,

who lived all her mental life, her real life, in a world
of daisy-chains and cherry-blossom and maypoles and
sun-bonnets, was born at, of all places, Hoxton, and
brought up at Islington ; and the passage described
how she and her sister would go out and explore Upper
Street, Islington, at evening, and find every shop-
window an Aladdin's Cave, and would lose themselves
in the wonders of street-corner entertainment, and
would give all the passing people, especially the
children better dressed than themselves, romantic life-
stories. And I thought of the High Street of another
suburb, where I had done the same, and of its autumn
evenings and shining shop-windows, and of myself
and Freda, both ten, walking home from Singing
Class ; and with that thought came a little train of
immortal hours set in that High Street.

Freda was the one who knew and understood. She
was at that time my only friend ; always there,
always understanding anything you said or half-said ;
always quiet and self-contained, yet with a simmer
of fun about eyes and lips ; always very ordinary, yet
always diffusing an aroma of extraordinary goodness.
This goodness was something she carried about with
her. It was invisible, yet it shone. It had nothing
to do with conduct. It was rather a wholeness of
being attached to no particular virtue but as much a
part of her as her dark hair, her white face and alert
violet eye. She had none of my own agitations and
uncertainties ; she was serene and acceptant—not
lymphatically but positively. Her face would, I suppose, have been called plain, but it was so constantly
filled with lights and curves of expression, little
crinkles of the nose or puckers of the lips or shadows
of the eye, that it was more attractive than most
pretty faces. She spoke always in the slow, soft tone
one uses at twilight, and her giggle, which came
rarely, had the sweetness of a smile.

We had been seeing each other in casual encounters,
and exchanging disjointed sentences, in the way of

children, for some time before we became friends.
Then, one night, coming home from Singing Class, our
perfunctory syllables took a dress of real talk, and our
haphazard acquaintance was made real companionship.

It was October. The weekly Singing Class evenings
and Magic Lantern evenings were for me special
evenings, not only as breaking the dull week but
because in winter they took me out After Dark, and
I always delighted in After Dark. I saw the streets
at different hours as possessed not only by people
and traffic and shops but by the spirit of those hours.
Morning gave everything a touch of its own special
quality; I couldn't name it but I knew what it was,
and that it was distinct from the quality given by
Afternoon. And Afternoon's quality or tinge was
quite other than that which displaced it and took
possession of the streets under the title of After Dark.

Being out After Dark was adventure. You were
in a wholly different world, a world that had things
in it which couldn't be seen in daylight. You could
plunge into it, as the heroes of Kingston and Ballan-
tyne plunged into purple forests or valleys of rock;
plunge into it and lose yourself. Each evening on
going out I was given an admonition—Mind-how-you-
cross-the-roads. That was all very well for cripples
and old people; for anybody else it was stuffy. I
liked to plunge into that bath of After Dark, and to
plunge into the High Street traffic under horses' heads,
and weave through lines of bicycles, and dodge hansoms, and come up breathless on the other side.

That evening the High Street, whose pulse for a son
of London beat always high with romance, was astir
with an extra rush of light and life. It was a scene
that came fresh to me each evening; the first sight
of it never failed to go tingling through me with the
bliss of music; and that evening the tingle was
notably keen. I had last seen it in the afternoon,
dressed in thin sun and mist. At that later hour it
was something new, washed and polished, like myself,

in its evening best, and making, with its glitter and
shine, a hospitable contrast with the windy waste of
the Green—a dark solitude of trees and ponds and
bushes that lay between the top of the High Street
and the next suburb. All the shops, great and small,
were in full doing, and the pavements were twinkling
with the in-and-out movements of shoppers and young
strollers, and the roadway was sending up a rumble
from carts, trams, buses and broughams, and there
was the jingle of harness-bells and the elfin artillery
of bicycle-bells. The main crowd moved about two
points at the centre of either side, and the bursts of
light at those points dazzled even the prodigal shops.
Those points were, on one side, the Imperial Palace of
Varieties, and on the other the Crystal Arcade, glass-
covered, fitted with white shops, lit by the new electric
light, and making a corridor of damask and pearl
between the High Street and the parish church.

Freda and I were walking home in the usual way
of children, sauntering, hastening, stopping. Freda's
walk was not the neat walk or lively skip of other
girls of her age. It was a series of leisurely lurches,
with her satchel swinging at full stretch of her arm,
untidy tassels of black hair being constantly thrown
back over her shoulder, her eyes looking anywhere
but where she was going, and her mind always somewhere else.

One of the features of my early life was the street-
organ. At that time it was everywhere, and certain
years, scenes, incidents and people became in my mind
dated, pointed by, and identified with a particular
song or air popular on the organs of the relative period.
The street-organ, as it were, set my life to music.
Almost every incident had a musical accompaniment.
Whatever happened, either at home or in the street,
somewhere a street-organ would be playing, and whatever it was playing fixed itself and the incident in my
mind as one. Thought of either carried thought of
the other, and to-day, when the radio revives certain

old songs, each of them annotates for me a particular year, and brings to me a scene, an incident, a person, an epoch of my interior life, and with it a host of related detail. My first encounter with Freda happened on the evening when I first joined the Singing Class. I saw her going down the side-street where it was held, and I asked her if she knew which building it was held in. She was wearing a blue frock at the time, and just as I spoke to her an organ struck up *Two Little Girls in Blue*, and she became fixed in my mind for ever with the air of that song.

On that October evening when we swung into friendship, our talk began with some remarks of mine on her piano-playing. This had been a revelation to me. The regular pianist for the Singing Class hadn't been able, that evening, to turn up, and to my surprise the singing-mistress had called upon Freda to deputise. Miss Sipsoe, she announced, was unable to be present owing to illness at home, and so, as we couldn't get on without music, somebody would have to make a special effort to take her place, and she would call on our Gifted Little Freda, who she was sure would be able to do it like anything. She did. I hadn't known of her accomplishments in that way, and I watched with some wonder as she got up with a quite casual air, lurched to the platform as though she were doing nothing unusual, and went through the job with an ease and assurance that changed my wonder to awe.

On the way home I was going to tell her how wonderfully clever I thought she was, and then it occurred to me that if she was wonderfully clever it would be wrong to find anything wonderful about it. So I only said : " I wish I could play the piano like you."

" Don't you play ? "

" No."

" Oh. . . . I thought everybody played the piano."
I felt at once incompetent and of little account.
" Why don't you learn ? "

" It costs money. And we haven't got a piano."

" I see."

" I'd like to be able to play like you. Did it take
you long to learn ? "

" I don't remember learning. I always seemed able
to. I've been playing ever since I did anything."

" D'you like playing ? "

" I don't know. Never thought about it. It comes
natural to me. That's what I'm going to Be."

" What ? "

" Pianist. Concert Pianist."

" Oh. . . ." I saw the prospect as already achieved,
and felt that I was in the presence of somebody from
a world beyond my range.

" Just now I help my Auntie. Accompanying her
when she's trying new songs. She's a singer."

" Oh. . . ." I was indeed in the presence of exalted
things, so I turned back to what I knew, and again
showed I knew little. " It must be splendid to
be able to play like you did this evening without
music."

" That ? Oh, that was nothing. Any six-year-old
could play that stuff. Just now I'm doing some of
the easier pieces of Mendelssohn and Schumann.
Later I shall go on to real things. Difficult things."

I didn't know about Mendelssohn and Schumann,
but I didn't say so. I switched. " D'you ever go
to Magic Lantern nights ? "

" No. I've heard about them. In the Geneva
Hall, aren't they ? "

" Yes. Just opposite where I live. Why don't you
come one evening ? "

" When are they ? "

" Every Thursday."

" Can't. That's my special practice night."

" What a pity. They're *lovely*. The colours ! "

" I love colour."

" So do I. Do you paint ? "

" A bit. I'm not good at it."

" I do a bit. And crayoning. I crayon Bible

B

texts—those blank ones they sell at Crawford's. I do them for my mother. And she frames them. And I copy things out of a book I've got called *Kate Green-away's Almanack*."

" I know. I've got one of those."

" Have you ? What colour d'you like best ? I like green and red."

We stopped, and she stood on one leg, swinging the other and swinging her satchel. " I like yellow, I think. Yellow and green and mauve."

" The Crystal Arcade," I said, " d'you like that ? "

" Oh, lovely. When I was five I used to think it was fairyland."

" I like the jeweller's window there."

" So do I."

" At home," I went on, spluttering in an unusual gush of talk, " we've got a big box of coloured beads. And often I've spent a whole evening just turning them over and staring at them."

" Yes. I know that feeling, looking at coloured things. You just go on looking and looking."

" I like looking at the fire, don't you ? Specially when it's wood and goes all green-and-blue like."

" I know." She lurched against me and cannoned off. " I've got a wall-paper in my room—all sorts of colours—and I lie in bed in the morning looking at it and making up things about it. All the colours seem different shapes. You know—brown's fat and green's thin and crimson's round and——"

I nodded in vigorous agreement. " I know. I've got a book at home with coloured pictures. Pictures of boys and girls doing things at home. And I know those rooms like I know our own. I'm not so in-terested in the bit shown in the picture but in the bits that aren't. The bits you can't see."

" Yes, I know. And you *can* see them."

" That's right. And when things are dull I sort of go and live in one of those rooms, and have fun with the boys, and go through the door on to the

landing, and go upstairs and downstairs. I know my
way all over that house."

" I've done that myself. But if you tell anyone
about it they think you're daft, and they jeer." She
made another lurch and another cannon.

" I know. I've never told anyone about it before.
Do you like games ? "

" Not outdoor games. And not any girls' games.
They're so soft."

" I don't either. Do you like school ? "

" Only some things. I like geography. And
history. Not much else."

" Those are what I like. Specially history. Not
about kings and battles. But about people. People
who did things."

" I like that too. My Auntie gave me a book on
my birthday about the lives of the composers. I've
read every page of it. All the things they did, and
the hard times they had. They were nearly all poor
—except Mendelssohn, and one or two who weren't
very great. Do you play cat's-cradle ? "

I didn't try to trace the connection of great composers and cat's-cradle. I just said " Yes."

" Let's play." She stopped under the lights of a
greengrocer's shop, and dived into her satchel and
brought out a string of coloured wool, and put her
satchel on the pavement, and we stood there in the
evening crowd and became engrossed in the perplexities
of cat's-cradle. While we were playing she said " It's
funny."

" What is ? "

" You and me. You seem just like me. Or I'm
just like you. We think like each other about a lot
of things. I've never met anybody before who did.
They're all so stuffy."

" Most of them are. And rude."

" Yes they are. They don't seem to understand
anything or see anything. You're different."

Most of us at any age like to be told that, and coming

from a deputy-pianist it was like an unexpected prize.
I blushed and giggled. She looked at me across the
network of cat's-cradle and giggled with me. The
giggle seemed to bring us together. It was like having
a precious secret.

When the cat's-cradle had reached its *dénouement*
she shoved the piece of wool back into her satchel, and
we strolled on into my home-street, the dim Geneva
Street. I went with her past our house, and on to the
middle of the street, where a narrow passage connected
it with her own Lamorna Road. That passage was
the draughtiest spot in our suburb. On windy days
one was blown through it; it always gave me the
fancy of walking through a trumpet while the bands-
man was playing it. We were blown through it that
night, and in a few seconds were out in Lamorna Road,
and it seemed that our brief exchange of confidences
was over. I didn't want it to be over; I wanted it
to go on. So instead of saying good night I lingered
and hesitated. We stood without saying anything,
staring down the lonely stretch of road, where the
lamps at our end were globes and disappeared in
some far dark country as pin-points. She stood
swinging one leg, and I stood kicking the kerb. At
last, as it was getting rather late, and as I thought she
might be wanting to get rid of me, I asked " Shall I
see you to-morrow ? "

" I expect so."

" When ? On the way to school ? "

" Yes. Perhaps."

" Shall I wait here at the corner ? "

" If you like."

" All right. I will. I——"

" What ? "

" I like you."

" I like you too."

And on that, which lit up and warmed the whole
night like a bonfire, we parted, and I ran home in that
state of glow which suffuses us at any time when we

meet the one congenial friend who speaks our language
and sees our fun.

.   .   .   .   .

We had the first floor of the house, and the landlady
and her family had the ground floor and the second
floor, so I knew what it felt like to be the ham in a
sandwich. But I was not aware of any pressure or
inconvenience. Those rooms had been my short lifetime's home, and I took all conditions for granted as
the natural order of things. Our living-room was a
room which was filled not quite with happiness, since
economic anxiety was always present, and not with
demonstrated affection, but with a consistent climate
of quiet tenderness and with a sense of security not
from worry but from all that was mean and hard. I
called it home, but it was more than that ; it was a
source and focus of the heart's light, and it was to
become a memory which, in the life of every man, is
of all memories the most perdurable. During the cold
months, whatever else might be wanting, it had always
a large fire beaming on it, and that fire was like a
reassuring and protecting guest telling us that things
weren't too bad.

When I got in the supper-table was set as usual by
the fire, and it held the supper of not-so-good weeks—
cocoa, biscuits and bread-and-butter pudding. Now
and then there was a surprise—sausages or sardines or
an egg on toast, or ham-and-tongue ; in summer,
fruits and cakes. Those were festal evenings. I never
expected them ; they came always with surprise ; and
I was never cast down by the everyday rice pudding
or bread-and-butter pudding. A phrase I had heard
in that room all through my ten years was " Blessed
is he that expecteth nothing," so I was always ready
to take what was there, and was not dismayed if it
wasn't.

The room was furnished with things that had once
been " good," and was as clean and precise in its

points as a dairy. I had to be the same. Geneva
Street had then no gas, and the room was lit by candle ;
the lamp was used only on Sundays or when visitors
came. The period was the 'nineties, but the contents
and atmosphere of the room were mainly of the 'sixties
and 'seventies. The mantel-shelf was a little museum
of the out-of-date—Bow china shepherds, lustres, vases
of Bohemian glass, odd Dresden cups and Worcester
saucers and scent-phials. The walls were dressed with
cheap prints of Birket Foster landscapes and with my
coloured texts. A hanging bookshelf held my library,
acquired as birthday or Christmas presents. It included *Robinson Crusoe, Grimm's Tales, The Young
Fur Traders, Ben-Hur, Coral Island, Sweet Stories of
Old, Black Beauty, Alone in London, Jessica's First
Prayer, Little Meg's Children, A Peep Behind the Scenes,
Last of the Mohicans, Carrots, Stories from the Faerie
Queen, Farthings*, and volumes of *Chatterbox* and *The
Scholar's Own ;* all in nineteenth-century bindings of
gaudy red or blue cloth, prodigally gilt on sides, back
and edges.

The supper-table was a sort of illustration of my
library, and made supper almost a meal of legend.
The coloured cloth was stamped with scenes from the
Lord Mayor's Show ; the plates were remnants of a
set whose centres bore designs based on *Uncle Tom's
Cabin ;* my cocoa cup and saucer were decorated with
coloured scenes from *Gulliver's Travels*, and the cocoa
jug bore spirited scenes based on Hans Andersen.

. . . . .

For three years Freda and I met almost every day,
often several times a day, but always on Saturday
mornings. Saturday Morning and Saturday Night
made points in my monotonous life. Saturday was
not a white-stone day of high pitch, like Christmas or
Easter, but it had a little more movement than everyday, and gave zest to my week. For one thing it was
a holiday. For another it was pocket-money day.

And again it had a quality and colour of its own—
a Saturday quality, genial and expansive. It was an
Uncle of a day where the other days were thin,
querulous Aunts. Saturday Morning meant always a
halfpenny to spend ; sometimes more. If a visitor
had called there might be a penny, and sometimes a
jam-jar produced yet another halfpenny or penny.

Saturday Morning brought always to our gay-
gardened little street a procession of picturesque vagabonds selling things, collecting things, or giving comic
performances or exhibitions of agility which had
neither beauty nor reason and yet created a sort of
poetry of the London street. Those I looked for were
not the performers or the sellers, but the collectors.
The first of these, as punctual as the clock, brought
into the street with trumpet and drum what looked
like a ship dressed for regatta or review. This was a
barrow piled high with stocks of paper windmills on
sticks, paper flags of all nations, and coloured air-
balloons. Any of those bright marvels could be had
in exchange for a jam-jar. But desirable as they were,
they did not appeal to me. I preferred money, and I
always waited for the barrow of the man who gave a
halfpenny for glass jam-jars and a penny for those of
earthenware. When I had one to sell, I would sometimes have as much as twopence to spend, and then
came the serious business of spending it, and I would
go off to the High Street.

Those Saturday Mornings were all of one pattern,
and followed the same procedure. One comes to me
at random ; one autumn Saturday when, thanks to
two visitors during the week and one glass jam-jar, I
sped away to the High Street with twopence-halfpenny.
Five halfpennies to spend, and the expectation of
seeing Freda, and a fresh misty morning in which the
ghost of summer lingered with a smile. On my way
to the High Street I passed two or three street-
performers going through their antics, but the thought
of my twopence-halfpenny so absorbed all my interest

that I did not even look at them. A street-organ was churning out *She Was a Dear Little Dicky-Bird*, and at the corner groups of my acquaintance were engaged in various singing-rituals of pastoral name—*Wall-flowers, Jenny is a-Weeping, I Sent a Letter to my Love, Mary in the Meadow*—folk-survivals from the village-greens of a thousand years ago, to which they had descended in tattered form from the religions of lost races of the Mediterranean.

All those street-games had their peculiar and un-accountable seasons. At a certain time of the year hoops would be brought out. For a month or so they would be in vogue ; then, as suddenly as they appeared, they would disappear and would be replaced by five-stones. Then five-stones would disappear, and marbles would be the thing, and again marbles would make way for peg-tops. And tops would pass, and singing-games would take their place. Nobody knew just when those seasons opened and closed. There was no sporting calendar in which their dates were set. There was no question of one or two children fixing on the First of May for marbles, and setting the fashion for the rest ; nor was there any unwritten but mutually-agreed code. It was something spontaneous which moved in the blood and set thousands of children, individually, in one particular week of the year, to produce marbles or whatever it might be, and moved them, again simul-taneously, in another week, to lay them aside and produce tops. It was such an instinct as moves a hundred individual apple-trees at one time to blossom, or moves a million individual swallows in the same week to make flight to the south.

I began my tour of the High Street shops at the station end, and worked up one side and down the other. They were then in a special mood, their Saturday Morning mood, and I lingered at each of them and was moved by the pictures they offered in their window-dressing to do my Saturday Morning shopping now here, now there. The baker's with its many styles and shapes of bread—the cottage loaf, the brick loaf, the tin loaf, the coburg, the Vienna Twist; the ham-and-beef shop with its glossy ox-tongues and brown roast chickens and glazed galantines and penny sausages in green and crimson and silver skins; the massed colours of the cakes and pastries in the confectioner's window, like a coloured plate in a stores catalogue; the florist's with its wonders of cups and bells and feathered crowns. With the flip of each door, as shoppers went in and out, I caught the odour peculiar to each shop—the earthiness of the greengrocer's, the warm reek of the florist's, the pungency of the chemist's, the piquancy of the grocer's, the solemnity of the draper's, the clean richness of the baker's, the harshness of the oil-and-colour shop. At those shops which had an outside show of cheap oddments, the greengrocer's, the toy-shop, the paper shop, I received a greeting. I sometimes spent two halfpennies with them, and the assistants knew me, so my progress up the street was a series of Morning Calls.

After I had toured both sides, I stood and debated what to do with my unusual store of money. I had no notion of saving part of it for Monday or Wednesday. Whatever my Saturday money, whether a halfpenny, a penny, or even what it was on that occasion, my way always was to dash it in one Saturnalia. The appeals were conflicting, the possibilities of choice bewildering, but I decided on a comic paper, sweets, biscuits, and something from the greengrocer. Each of those, in its turn, offered various sub-attractions. Of comic papers you could get for a halfpenny *Comic Cuts*, *Chips* or the *Funny Wonder*. At the big confectioner's you could get three of yesterday's pastries for a penny, or at the grocer's a big bag of broken wafers for a half-penny. At the greengrocer's were oranges, bananas, chestnuts and pomegranates. Oranges were four a penny; bananas three a penny; pomegranates two a penny; and for a penny they would give you a capful

of chestnuts. The pomegranate wasn't very satisfying
or delicious in the eating, but it was a lovely word to
bring out, and it was a lovely thing to hold and look
at—the polished brown-gold of its rind, and its odd
shape, and the gorgeous colour of its inside. I
hesitated on the common pleasure of the orange, the
glossy look of chestnuts and the fun of roasting them
on the fire-bars, and the varied appeals of the pomegranate ; and I knew that when I had decided and
had made my purchase I would wish I had made some
other.

At the sweets shop the problem was more intense ;
the possibilities reached almost the hundred. Almond-
rock had a finer flavour than coconut-toffee, but you
got only two ounces of almond-rock for a penny,
while you got four ounces of coconut-toffee ; and of
that mixture of sweets called all-sorts a penny bought
six ounces. And there were all the other things—
clove-stick, locusts, sugar-candy, coconut-ice, bull's-
eyes, bouncers, brandy-balls, Chinese cushions,
liquorice-strips, Chicago caramels, Jap nuggets, Ponte-
fract comfits, crystallised-chips, coconut nib-stick, pop-
corn, barley-sugar, colt's-foot-rock, marzipan, burnt
almonds. Of some of the humbler of those the smaller
shops would serve farthing's-worths. In summer you
could get for a halfpenny a glass of sherbet and water,
and in winter a hot fruit-drink, and there were other
tempting things than those for the stomach.

There were prize-packets. There were transfers
with their opulent colours, a halfpenny a sheet. At a
halfpenny there were little glass-lidded boxes containing a tortoise made of gelatine ; when you set the box
on the palm of your hand the head and legs wiggled.
Again at a halfpenny you could get a box of coloured
matches which burnt with flames of red and blue and
green. Still at a halfpenny you could get a butterfly,
five sizes larger than life, made of some gauze material ;
that, too, went on the palm of your hand whose warmth
set it performing realistically the movement of opening

and closing its wings. For a halfpenny again you could get a toy pistol, and at another halfpenny a box of " caps " ; or a large cardboard bumble-bee, with elastic wound about it, and a long piece of string to it, by which you whirled it round your head and caused it to give a convincing hum. Or you could get twelve " throwdowns," little twists of paper of various colours containing a pinch of some explosive substance ; you flung them to the ground, preferably behind an elderly man, and they gave a report like that of a Chinese cracker.

After mature consideration I acquired at four different shops the *Funny Wonder*, an ounce of coconut-toffee, a clove-stick, a prize-packet, and a bag of broken wafers, and then carried the remnant coin to the greengrocer's for chestnuts, a pomegranate or two small oranges. The greengrocer's Saturday window was usually the show of the street. There were pyramids of blackberries, hills of Jaffa oranges, boxes of silvered tangerines, cromlechs of shining apples, festoons of grapes as large as plums, fields of walnuts, Brazil nuts and filberts, and scarlet borders of cranberries. But the glories of the window were not for me ; my ground was the outside stall ; and I finally made a plunge and decided on chestnuts, and for my halfpenny got half a capful, with another two for luck because (I was told) of the twinkle in my eye. And so my twopence-halfpenny was spent :

Funny Wonder	$\frac{1}{2}d.$
Prize-packet	$\frac{1}{2}d.$
1 oz. coconut-toffee	$\frac{1}{4}d.$
Clove-stick	$\frac{1}{4}d.$
Bag of wafers	$\frac{1}{2}d.$
Chestnuts	$\frac{1}{2}d.$
	$2\frac{1}{2}d.$

And then Freda gave me a push in the back—her usual salute if she came behind me—and stood and giggled. She was not, as I said, the giggling sort, but always at first sight of me she giggled, though it was more gurgle than giggle. She seemed to regard me as some subtle joke of her own making, and I never could retaliate. I wasn't in a position to exhibit male assertion over a girl who was a deputy-pianist.

" Hullo."

" Hullo. Where you going ? "

" Nowhere."

" Have some almond hardbake ? " She dived into her satchel and produced two packets and offered one to me. Almond hardbake, I knew, was a halfpenny a packet, and I hesitated. " Go on, silly. Take it." Then I remembered that she had a father, and got as much as sixpence a week pocket-money ; so I took it. " Have a mulberry ? " She dived again into the satchel and out came a bag of mulberries. That satchel of hers was for me one of life's mysteries. Always she was diving into it and producing from it, like a conjurer, the most unlikely things—bits of coloured wool, music, mulberries, ice-cream wafers, sticking-plaster, nail-scissors, drawing-pins, toffee that had melted, squashed flowers, a piece of stained glass, dried seaweed, curtain-rings, a pastry-cutter, a thermometer, the dial of a broken clock, a mandolin plectrum, a baby's rattle, a magnet, and even schoolbooks. Often I wanted to have a good look at it, and go right through it, but I felt it would be a sort of sacrilege even to ask such a thing of a girl.

I produced my purchases. " Have a wafer ? "

" Not now."

I was glad she didn't want one of my wafers, and in the same moment I was ashamed I was glad. " Have a prize-packet ? "

" No, thanks. Daddy brought me one yesterday."

" Have some coconut-toffee ? "

" Yes, I'll have some of that."

" How can we break it—on the wall ? "

" Wait a minute. I know." Into the satchel again,

and out came a pair of pliers. With them we broke
the toffee into pieces, and then went, all sticky, up the
High Street, and I entertained her by making up
fantastic and inconsequent life-stories for the people
looking in the shop-windows. She was flattering
enough to find the stories wonderful, and to be unable
to think how I did it. At the top of the High Street
she asked, " Did you get any samples this morning ? "

" Samples " was a new game to which she had
introduced me and which gave me the adult dignity of
a regular postal delivery of my own. At that time
manufacturers did their business on a personal and
humane basis, and tried to outdo each other in their
bounty to potential customers. At the cost of a halfpenny postcard you could get free samples of all sorts
of useful or interesting things, and as Freda's home
always had a stock of stamped postcards she shared
them with me, and we made a pastime of looking
through all the papers and magazines we could get
hold of and " writing up " for samples and catalogues,
and comparing and exchanging the results. For your
postcard you could get samples of tea, of cocoa, of
coffee-essence and fruit drinks ; samples of metal
polish, of note-paper, or pen-nibs, tooth-paste, and
baking-powder. Advertisers sent not only these
samples of their goods, but little treasures for the
children. Many of the free gifts were enchanting
puzzles of wire or cardboard, or little toys, or knick-
knacks, or booklets of fairy-tales or nursery-rhymes
bearing the name of the advertiser's product. And
there were the thick and gorgeously coloured Christmas
catalogues of the big stores, better than any fairy-
tales. I sent for them all, and some weeks I had such
a post that the postman must have thought I was
setting up as a general dealer.

It was an age of free gifts. Shops, too, gave things
away. At Christmas they gave giant air-balloons of
variegated colours. At ordinary times they gave with
a pair of children's boots a twelve-inch school ruler,

with a boy's suit a pencil-box, with a school-satchel a note-book, each gift stamped with the shopman's name. Tradesmen gave Christmas boxes. From the milkman came a jug of cream ; from the grocer a box of sugared biscuits, from the baker, flour, from the greengrocer a box of dates, and children at their regular sweet-shop received a free hot drink. At the annual trade exhibitions at the Agricultural Hall, the Dairy Exhibition, the Grocers', the Bakers' and Confectioners', all exhibitors gave free samples, and one could attend them with a shopping basket and bring it home full to the top and live for a week on it. It was a pretty custom, the Free Sample custom, but it belongs now in the list of the superannuated.

I answered Freda with " Yes. I got a specimen number of a new boys' paper and a little jar of potted meat. Did you get anything ? "

" Yes. I got the scent I wrote for—a lovely little bottle about an inch high. And on Thursday I got two tiny tablets of soap and a little packet of biscuits."

" I had something on Thursday too—a little pot of honey, Gamage's catalogue, and a little bottle of Tumcura—the thing they advertised in your mother's paper. Only it isn't a drink. It's a cure for something they call heartburn. I don't know what that is."

" What did you do with it ? "

" I poured it down the sink. I'll lend you Gamage's catalogue. It's lovely."

" All catalogues are, I think."

When we reached the white-railed Green we wandered round the ponds, where boys from the poorer quarter were trawling with towels for stickle-backs, and the solemn children of the prosperous Grove quarter were solemnly parading with their nurses. There we stood and stared, and discussed Life and its problems.

The Green, though a part of London, gave a quite sharp illusion of the rural. Our suburb had on show all the public up-to-date things—trams, buses, station-cabs, music-hall, Italian café, Salmon & Gluckstein,

Home & Colonial Stores, Freeman, Hardy & Willis—
but in its private life it was forty or fifty years behind
the time. Away from the High Street it was not
progressive, and had the air of not wanting to be. In
the High Street it accepted the *fin-de-siècle* mode and
paraphernalia, but elsewhere, in thought and habit, it
lived at its own tempo and in its own dress. Round
the Green it had Queen Anne houses and middle-
Georgian and Regency houses, and in the minor
shopping streets the shops had modern fronts aproned
on to buildings that had been new about the time of
Trafalgar. At the point where the High Street met
the Green it made a bend, and continued itself as a
more select and expensive High Street under the name
of the Old Road. This was a clean and sunny stretch,
facing the Green, and bright with dainty little shops,
all sun-blinds and silken dusky interiors, offering the
higher confectionery, the finer fruit, perfumes, fabrics,
flowers. There the High Street's modern pace would
have been a discord. There custom was cool and
leisured, and there it seemed to be always summer
afternoon in an old story.

Off the High Street were many little still-rural nooks
—Squares, Rows, Places, Circuses—with weather-board
houses and red blinds and long front gardens happy
and unashamed with such weedy beauties as corn-
flowers, marigolds, nasturtiums, convolvulus, creeping-
jenny and musk. Those nooks had a self-sufficient
life of their own; their own shops and their own
belated customs. In one of them was even a dairy-
farm with cows, from which each afternoon I fetched
our milk. They had no ovens to their fires, and a
regular Sunday-morning spectacle was the procession
of children carrying the joints and pies to be cooked
at the local baker's at a fee of one penny per
dish.

It was Our Village, and it had something of village
life. London is not one great city; it is a homogeneous
assembly of a number of small towns and hamlets,

each helping to compose London but each, at that time, retaining its individual character and way of life. Our Village, like a real village, had its ranks and dignities, and the people of both the prosperous quarter and the very poor quarter were of old-established family. Those who lived in the Queen Anne and Georgian houses and in the expensive Grove, and those who lived in the weather-board cottages, were living in the houses where their grandfathers and great-grandfathers had lived. Their homes had been on the rate-books of that parish in days before anybody had heard the name of Napoleon. The Grove quarter made ostentation with broughams and victorias and cockaded coachmen ; it was known as the quarter of the Carriage Folk, a term which was a classification ; I suppose on the Probert principle of identifying social eminence with gigs. In the quiet streets leading from the Green the note was of penurious " gentility." The other sections ranged from comfortable middle-class down through shabby genteel and ignoble decency to slapdash poor.

As we leaned over the rails of one of the ponds, chewing toffee, we could see nothing but a distance of grass and elms, and beyond them an occasional tinge of the red brick of the Queen Anne houses. After a long silence Freda said, " I like autumn mornings, don't you ? Everything smells silver. Wet and silver."

" I know."

" Do you ever cry ? "

" Not when I'm hurt. Boys don't."

" No, of course not. I don't mean that. I never cry when I'm miserable. But I do sometimes. I cried myself to sleep last Christmas Eve."

" Whatever for ? "

" I don't know. Only—when I went up to bed there was a full moon and it was cold and there was snow on the roofs and the sky was green and I could see the High Street lights and it was Christmas Eve and——"

"I know what you mean. The organ sometimes makes me feel like that."

"The church organ?"

"No, silly. The street-organ. Specially when it's playing comic songs."

"I think I know what you mean. It's funny, isn't it?"

"No. I don't think it's funny. There must be a reason for it. I expect somebody clever could explain it."

"Yes. There's lots of things that make you stop thinking, aren't there? You can't get any farther. I feel it sometimes when I'm playing. And sometimes at home, though most times I love them all, there's other times when I feel I'm among a lot of strangers. As though I don't belong to them. And I wonder what I'm doing there, as though I'd got into the wrong house. And I try to think it out, and I can't. It's just one of the funny things that you have to give up."

"I've felt it sometimes."

"I wonder whether others do?"

"I expect so. Only they wouldn't like to tell. I wonder why grown-up people make everything so dull. Specially when one feels excited about things. And there's such a lot of exciting things, aren't there?"

"Yes. All sorts of things. I feel rather sorry for them. They seem afraid of getting excited in case they look silly. And so they get dull. And they make everything like themselves. They spread it about. Even the nicest things get dull by being near them. I hope I shan't grow up like them, and spoil everything the way they do."

"They do. There's a house we go to sometimes— got lovely things in it. At least, they'd be lovely if they were anywhere else. But because they're in that house they look dull—just having to live with those people."

"I know. There's a piece of music I've always

c

loved. But I can't play it any more. I had to play
it once to some of Daddy's stuffy old friends, and they
said such silly dull things about it, they spoiled it for
me. I've never played it since. There seems more
dull people about than lively ones."

" Yes. I wonder why they make everything so
miserable. They *look* miserable. They make work
miserable and they make fun miserable. Always
saying you mustn't get excited."

" My Auntie says it's because they think too much.
That's why artists, she says—you know, poets and
musicians and people who paint and write books—are
so much happier than other people. 'Cos they don't
think too much. They enjoy everything and don't
bother over silly troubles like ordinary people. Auntie
says thought's a kind of poison. Like bad air.
Wherever it gets to, it turns things bad. Thinking,
she says, never makes things any better. It only
makes nice things not so nice. Things are what they
are, she says, when they first happen, before you think
about them, and they're nearly all good then. If you
start thinking, they don't seem so good. I must run
now. I've got to go to practice."

" I'd like to hear you play sometime. Some of the
real music you spoke about."

" You can if you like. Any time. I go to my
Auntie's usually—her piano's better than ours. But
I'm nothing. You ought to hear *her*."

" I'd rather hear you. Does she live near here ? "

" Yes. Up there, in the Grove."

" One of those big houses ? "

" Mmm. She makes quite a lot of money. She's
always singing somewhere. I'll get her to sing to you
one day. She's glorious. And she's lovely to look
at, too. Not a bit like Mummy."

" I only want to hear you play—first. You've
never played when I've come to tea."

" I can't when the others are about. I can't do
proper playing. They make fun, and cackle. They

think I'm showing off. But it's twelve o'clock. I really must go. See you to-morrow, I expect."

And she swung away from the rails, and shot across the Green with satchel whirling in the air ; shot along with the ecstasy of a kitten and the graceless grace of a colt ; and I strolled home to Geneva Street and the bright fire, where the visitation of the wandering merchants was still in progress. One by one they passed along the narrow street with their gay or sombre carts, filling the air with those cries which now are stilled—cries of Coal and Milk and *Old Moore's Almanack,* of Salt and Logs and Nuts and the local *Gazette,* and All a-Blowing and Chairs-to-Mend and Knives-to-Grind and Hearth-brooms, with the bell of the muffin-and-crumpet man to punctuate them. Though the cries told you nothing of the wares unless you knew the Eskimo language of Street Cries. You had to know that Myo-koo meant milk ; that Whur-ho meant coals ; that Pur meant the *Gazette ;* that Gran-hoo meant Knives-to-Grind ; that Ah-Boo meant Hearth-brooms, and that Cheer-Up meant Chairs-to-Mend.

The event of Saturday Morning was repeated and amplified by Saturday Night. The High Street then was again a different High Street. Shops which on other nights closed at ten were open till midnight, and they were Saturday Night shops, with mood and movement heightened and accelerated. The butcher's straw hat and blue apron were those he always wore, but they assumed an air of carnival. The greengrocer's chanted invitation was not purely commercial ; that, too, held a ring of festival. The whole street indeed seethed with a rich and fruity flush of life, charged to the overflow with the spirit of English Saturday Night. To the shop-lights of orange or lemon were added the white flares of the naphtha-lamps of the stalls and all their hot noise. There were the oyster-stall (oysters 6d. a dozen) ; the sweets stall where sweets were made on the cramped premises ; the baked-potato stall ;

the sarsaparilla stall ; the saveloy and pease-pudding
stall ; the colporteur's stall, descendant of the seventeenth-century chapman or flying stationer, with
religious booklets and texts ; the toy stall ; the cough-
lozenge stall. At every corner was an entertainment
—the Calculating Horse ; a nigger troupe ; a Bran
Pie ; a German Band ; a Salvation Army meeting.
On vacant spaces there would be a contortionist, a
Highland sword-dancer, a thought-reader, a phren-
ologist, a one-man band. There were Italian women
in Neapolitan costume, with a cage of budgerigars
which were supposed to tell your fortune by picking
out with their beaks one card from a pack of fortune
cards. And there was my favourite—the Peep Show.
This was a glass-fronted box, and for a halfpenny the
man would remove the cover from the window and
would touch a spring, and you saw a model village in
which everything was alive. The trees waved, the
cattle nodded their heads, cottage doors opened and
figures slid to the threshold, water ran down the mill-
wheel, the windmill sails revolved, the grinding-stone
revolved, and a figure at the pump worked its handle
and it gushed real water. It was a ha'porth of poetic
experience. In between the stalls were beggars or
cripples with matches, bootlaces, silly toys ; and
there were cheerful voices and light scuffles of feet
around the Imperial Palace and the Crystal Arcade
and the Italian café ; and in the roadway through day
and darkness the traffic rumbled and jingled.

And back home, at supper-time, when the street was
still, there would yet be a late organ to send up to our
windows the grievous tunes of London comic songs—
tunes so charged with the self-mocking pathos of the
London streets that they might have been the spirits
of dead Londoners made into music.

CHAPTER III

OLD-TIME SUBURB

AS I stood staring at the Kate Greenaway picture it dissolved into still more pictures of the old suburb ; not perhaps as others saw it but as I saw it with child's eyes and as it lived in my heart. I had for it in those years that feeling that grows from daily use, which leads to memories, which in turn lead to love. And love, far from being blind, gives us what intellect cannot give. For human vision it gives us divine vision. The eyes of the mind are dim. The eyes of love are clear and open. So those common and often shabby places which were the settings of our youth show their true selves only to the unclouded sight of our love.

Our suburb was, as I say, conservative, and in a world of change it still is. After an absence of some decades I took recently the risk of seeing it again. I made the sometimes painful experiment of going back, and the pain was not, as it often is, in the fact that everything had changed and the old magic evaporated, but in the fact that it *hadn't* ; that it was still there ; that the phantoms of my youth rushed up at me from every corner and made the journey one long ache. They rushed up in such tumult that I did not dare even to glance down the length of Geneva Street for fear others would rush from there and clutch my heart with so many fingers that they would arrest it. I kept to the High Street. And there I found what I think could be found in no other suburb. I found the past in such full current of being that there seemed to be no past. Though it was as modern as other High Streets, with cinemas, ice-rink, fun-fair, dance hall and tea-shops, I found some twenty shops with the same fronts bearing the names they had borne fifty years ago.

The pictures that lived in my heart were living still in substance. There was the bow-fronted Regency shop of the chemist ; the stationer's shop with the flight of steps, where I bought my first box of crayons ; the baker's where I had bought yesterday's pastries ; the toy-shop in the Crystal Arcade, just as it was when it materialised for me each year the idea of Christmas ; the bookseller's where I bought my first real books ; the tobacconist's where at fourteen I bought my first cigarettes—Ogden's Guinea Gold, $2\frac{1}{2}d$. for ten ; the coffee-blender's, gushing the same rich aroma by which even the blind match seller could guess where to take his stand ; and the chief confectioner was still filling his window with his great five-tier Christmas cake as he had done these fifty years. They were all there, and with the same old names, like an index to the chapters and pages of my heart.

Yet they seemed unearthly, so remote from my present life that it was as though I had somehow got into the scenes and among the characters of some novel I had been reading. I could not see them as part of the common London of to-day. They seemed to exist only as a backcloth from an old pantomime, behind which some transformation scene was preparing ; they were so linked not only with my fact-life but with my dreams. And to-day I cannot disentangle fact from dream. All sorts of strange and moving things happened to me in that High Street, but I cannot now say certainly of any episode whether it was fact or dream, or partook of both, since both were equally intense experiences. I know I went in and out of those shops when I was six and seven and ten, in fact and in dream, but that boy seems a separate being, a phantom of my own dreams. Between him and me, and between me and those shops, came the long severance of adolescence, and I see him as some boy with whom I was acquainted and who permitted me to enter his mind and follow his thoughts and his reveries. Looking at the names over those shops I found myself wondering whether the life since those days had been a dream, or whether all that past life was as much a dream as the shops seem to be to-day. And I felt that my first conjecture was right. That boy is still about, and often I am aware of him. I find him following me through my present dream, following me as my shadow, watching me, laughing privately at things I do and say, keeping a sort of amused guard over me while I play at being grown up and pretend not to see him.

At that time the suburb was so conservative that though it was a London suburb it had a squire who appeared every morning on the Green on horseback. It had several Lady Bountifuls and many a rustic wit. And it observed many old and now obsolete customs. It had ballad-singers who sang the ballads (pirated copies of the verse of music-hall songs) which they sold at six a penny. It held fairs on Bank Holidays. On May Day it had the chimney-sweeps' procession with Jack-in-the-Green. It had simnel cakes at Easter, and at Whitsun it had parades of the Friendly Societies and of the tradesmen's cart-horses. For the Boat Race all boys wore light or dark blue favours in their coats or caps—usually a small velvet monkey. Grottoes were built in July by children who knew nothing of St. James of Compostella, and in November elaborate guys were carried round the streets by men as well as boys, and every little back-garden had its own display of fireworks, and every little sweetstuff shop made its window gay with those explosive trifles whose names are rich wrappings for richer wonders—Bengal Lights, Jewel Fountains, Roman Candles, Chinese Trees, Catherine Wheels, Fiery Whirlwinds, Golden Rain.

A minor festival peculiar to South London was that of Derby Night, when we lined the High Street and cheered the procession of decorated vehicles from the noble to the ridiculous, the staid to the eccentric. It was an annual pageant that had survived without a

break from the days of the Regency. Four-in-hands,
victorias, landaus, wagonettes, hansoms, dog-carts,
traps, milk - floats, vans, donkey - barrows — they
streamed from south to north, while on the pavement
hawkers sold air-balloons of red and blue and green,
and water-squirters, and ticklers, and bags of confetti,
and between pavement and roadway went a constant
fire of that rude badinage which is the open air's uncut
wit. In summer, every Sunday night made a small
copy of this carnival with a procession of brakes and
wagonettes returning from a communal day in the
country, cornet or concertina going at full strength and
the company singing choruses. And on Wednesday
evenings during the light months a band on the Green
made the air gay and golden with Sousa's Marches and
Waldteufel's Waltzes.

Old age then came to people much earlier than it
does to-day. At a time when the grandmother of
to-day is going to dances, women of the same age were
" old ladies " in lace caps. An unmarried woman of
thirty was " on the shelf." At fifty-five men retired
from business and put on smoking-caps and sat back.
In Parliament beards were grey at an age which to-day
ranks a man as " one of the younger men." Bald
heads were as common as advertisements of hair-
restorers. Some of the older women of the Grove
district still dressed their hair with chignons, and went
about in Indian shawls or dolmans. Bonnets were
still worn, and phaetons were used, and governess-
carts. Wax flowers under glass shades, and boxes of
sea-shells were to be seen in the homes of rich as well
as poor. *L'art nouveau* had not reached our suburb,
not even its advanced set—if it had one.

We had one large modern public-house which called
itself a hotel, and several little old taverns that had
forgotten how time passes and how one ought to keep
up with it ; low, small-windowed snuggeries with
sanded floors and scrubbed benches and wide fireplaces,
where the great-great-grandfathers had sat and gos-

siped. Our transport was that of most other suburbs of the time. For three-halfpence horse-trams of different colours carried us to the bridges ; a chocolate tram to Westminster, a red tram to Waterloo, a green tram to Blackfriars. A halfpenny bus carried us across each bridge. The drivers of the trams stood on open platforms exposed to all weathers. They took their meals, which seemed to be mainly cans of hot tea, while driving. Conductors announced in loud voices the destination of trams and buses. We could stop a tram at any point at which we wanted to get on or off, but the right thing was to jump on or off without stopping it. If we wanted to travel in any other direction than the bridges we walked until we came to some other highway where we could pick up bus or tram, and we didn't mind walking—we were that rustic.

Most tram drivers and bus drivers, and all policemen and firemen wore beards. The bus drivers wore glazed top-hats and tarpaulin capes, and in summer straw hats. Hansom-cab drivers wore regular driving coats and silk hats whose silk had long departed.

The price of things in those far-off days seems rather of fairyland than of our England. We are told that the present cost of living is only about ninety per cent. above that of the beginning of the century. In the matter of food, the figure may be accurate. But on the whole the increase is about four hundred per cent. ; to do to-day what you could then do with a golden sovereign would need quite four of our paper pounds. At that time the poorer people could get a six-room villa in a decent road for £30 a year including rates. They could get a decent suit or costume for three or four pounds. Letter-postage was a penny for four ounces ; postcards a halfpenny. The best " drawing-room " coal was thirty shillings a ton. Eggs were fourteen for a shilling. A serviceable watch could be had for five shillings. Irish linen handkerchiefs were three shillings a dozen. In springtime violets were a

penny a bunch, and strawberries in June were fourpence
a pound.

I have shown what a child in my own sphere could
buy for a halfpenny, and the prices of things of every
kind were proportionate, so that the people who lived
in the Grove district were able to live in solidly comfortable style on a thousand a year. The number of
things to be had for a penny was uncountable ; a
music-hall song of the period was devoted to celebrating
that phenomenon, and advantage was taken of it
commercially by the establishment in most suburbs,
including ours, of Penny Bazaars.

There was even penny entertainment. I don't mean
the Penny Gaff. That had been suppressed many
years earlier. I mean something much less ragged
—and less popular : the anæmic Penny Reading.
Younger people will not have heard of the Penny
Readings, and even the middle-aged who were born in
comfortable circumstances will not know them. They
were not produced for the well-to-do. They were an
expression of that philanthropic, parsonic, patronising
attitude to the poorer people, and their purpose was
to keep those people from enjoying the impious delights
and polluting atmosphere of the theatre and the
music-hall. By the 'nineties they were in most places
as extinct as their coarse brother, the Penny Gaff, but
in the conservatism of our suburb they survived. The
Church people who ran them deluded themselves with
the notion that they were still a vogue. The vogue
was not clamant, and the good work they were supposed
to do was not apparent ; the Imperial Palace almost
every night had to turn money away. At the only
Penny Reading to which I was taken—I refused to be
taken to a second—the church hall in which it was
given held no more than twenty people.

The specimen I attended was, I learned, typical of
all. It was conducted by one of the Lady Bountifuls,
assisted by those hardworking males and females who
seem to be all of one sex and are known as Church

Workers. Lady Bountiful did the job with the air of
a magnanimous giraffe. She wore pince-nez which
she had difficulty in keeping on, and so held her head
back and looked at us very much down the nose.
While announcing the items she ambled up and down
the platform, just like the Zoo's giraffe, restless in its
paddock. She was tall, and her withdrawn head and
high coiffure suggested to my fancy that she could
easily take her food off the lintel of the platform door
like any other giraffe. She used the breaks between
each item, before announcing the next, as opportunities
for little homilies on what she called Temperance,
which seemed to mean that you must never, never, at
any time, take as much as a sip of Strong Drink.

The show was opened by her daughter, who gave a
reading from *A Christmas Carol*. Then a curate went
on to the platform, with a playful skip, and gave us
one of George Rose's *Mrs. Brown* papers. Before
announcing the next turn Lady Bountiful, glaring at
us with an expression of arctic fraternity, and thrusting
at us with her forefinger, as though prodding the
inattentive in a tender spot, spoke of rational entertainment and how it could be enjoyed without the adjunct
of Strong Drink. She referred to the number of people
whom Strong Drink had brought to a bad end. She
glanced at the world's strongest men—Hercules, Samson, Blondin, Sandow—and remarked that they were
all water-drinkers. An impertinent enquiring spirit,
a small girl sitting near me, piped up and asked
whether Samson didn't come to a bad end. She got a
glare and a thrust, and was answered in a breath
with " Yes-Cissie-but-not-through-strong-drink-and-
don't-interrupt."

Then a churchwarden gave us a reading from Mark
Twain, and that was followed by a German-Reed
drawing-room sketch performed by the curate and
Lady Bountiful herself. At the next interval, after
two boys had given a scene from *Henry V*, she told us
of her grandmother, and how, in her last illness, the

doctor said that a little brandy might help, but the old lady said No; Strong Drink had never passed her lips, and never should; and she died true to the Blue Ribbon, and happy would it be for all of us if we could be as staunch. Again the impertinent enquiring spirit piped up and wanted to know if that meant that it would be happier for us if we were dead, and was given a glare of flaming ice and a " Now-Cissie ! " that made her duck behind a chair and silenced her for ever.

Then one of the Church Workers gave us *John Gilpin*, and when he had done, Lady Bountiful led an unsupported demand for an encore, and he gave *The Bell of the Inchcape Rock* when I was hoping for *The Fireman's Wedding*. Then the daughter gave us Tennyson's *Victim*, and the evening wound up in what should have been hilarity with a reading by the choir-master, in a voice suited to a reading of the Litany, from *Valentine Vox*.

The church and religion pervaded all my childhood years. Our circle " went in " for religion—a senti-mentalised religion—as other circles went in for foot-ball. But all it meant to me was the sad Sahara of Sunday, and doleful bells, and the sluggard moan of hymns, and the suffocating odour of kid gloves. I hated Sundays and those bells and the kid-glove odour of churches and the unhappy hymn-tunes ; yet, since things absorbed in childhood become for ever part of us and make a cherished corner for themselves, so at this day any Sunday morning, any sound of doleful bells, any of those hymn-tunes caught from an open church door have the power to knock at the heart and compel an answer of smiling recognition.

As the crystallisation of all those things I recall the owner of one of the Queen Anne houses of the Grove, of whose bright garden and meadow I was free. I see her chiefly as a black silk dress, lace cape, white hair and white hands, and every evocation of that image has a silvery edge. She and all that touched her, her

voice, her opinions, everything that was where she
was, took something of the lustre of old silver. The
very daylight of her rooms seemed tempered to silver.
Even her servants had it, and in their speech and
movements emitted a silvern ether.

Those were the days of servants. She was one lone
woman, and to minister to her simple wants she had
personal maid, cook, housemaid, parlourmaid, daily
charwoman, gardener and coachman. Having nothing
to do, and not being strong enough for much visiting
or entertaining, she cultivated religion and benevolence
—the latter without any inconvenience to herself.
Her benevolence was merely a matter of giving orders
to the servants. In summer every tradesman's boy
who came to the kitchen door was offered a glass of
iced barley-water, and in winter a cup of cocoa and
biscuits. To the sick poor the servants carried baskets
of invalid nourishment. At Christmas each tradesman's boy was given a " parcel," and working upwards
from tradesmen's boys the scale of benevolence in-
creased in proportion to the needs of those whose needs
she knew, until the servants were worked to the point
of mild protest. Orders went out for blankets, dresses,
boots, coals, children's clothes and groceries as if from
a municipal institution—all to be packed and dis-
tributed by the servants.

The atmosphere of placid piety which accompanied
the old lady's every act and speech, tedious as I found
it then, has in retrospect the charm of an antique. It
suffused house and garden, and gave sunny peace to
both. Every day in that house seemed to be Sunday
morning ; you could almost hear the bells and smell
the kid gloves. No inmate of that house had ever
been to a theatre or even a concert. None of them
had tasted Drink. When they went out, mistress or
maids, it was only to church or for a quiet walk or
drive, or to carry one of those bountiful baskets. I
never saw a newspaper or any secular literature in that
house ; only in the drawing-room the *Church Times*

and the parish magazine, and for the servants the
Cottager and Artisan and *Home Chimes*.

Years later I perceived that piety was as natural to
her as genius to a genius. It was her *métier*. She
made something positive of it, so that when you were
with her you felt that you really were in the presence
of the indefinable peace. She had never heard of the
Higher Criticism, and if she had been told about it
she would not have " heard " of it. She had such a
capacity for belief that the most fabulous Old Testament stories might have been a crew of Jonahs and
she the swallowing whale. Even *Hymns Ancient and
Modern* were for her part of the divine utterance. All
was true, and because she believed it to be so it filled
her days and her house with benediction.

I understood this, but without sympathy, and once
or twice, with the audacity or bad manners of the child,
I attempted argument. I wanted to know why she
was so certain of what she said. I couldn't see any
reason for such certainty ; not knowing at that time
that these matters are outside reason. We never got
very far. I couldn't accept her flat statement that it
was all in the Book, and she dismissed my ideas of
what life might be. Life, she held, was a Vale of Woe
in which we were doing penance. We were burdened
with sin and must suffer accordingly, though, if we
contrived to cleanse ourselves with good works, we
might eventually be forgiven and promoted to that
abode of bliss above the bright blue sky. I said I was
sure that most people weren't burdened with sin, and
I couldn't see why I should be expected to kneel down
and say I was a miserable sinner when I wasn't ; or
grovel to some awful angry power for mercy when I
hadn't done any wrong. I asked why the religious
made life so miserable if they really believed their own
story of a loving father, and she fumbled, and then
hedged, and said this world and the Kingdom were
two different things. Which sounded at first as though
it meant something, and then sounded like syllables.

Always in argument, I found, one's elders would escape via syllables. To childhood life throws up every week a dozen insoluble problems demanding answers from the apparently enlightened, and the apparently enlightened have nothing to offer but syllables. I never in any way was tormented by my religious doubts ; I never wanted anything to cling to ; but I was often tormented by little secular puzzles of everyday. Phrases and public notices in the streets and shops gave me hours of private worry. I worried for days and nights to discover why we were said to Sit Up Late when on those occasions we were most of the time standing. I was puzzled too by those confectioners' shops which recommended their cakes by the announcement that they were Home Made. I could not see why cakes made at home should be superior to those made elsewhere, and I wanted to ask the confectioners how many homes they knew, because I knew *some* homes whose cakes . . . Other shops puzzled me by offering to put a new cover on your umbrella While You Wait. I could not see how it could be done otherwise, since if you wanted anything of that kind done you always had to wait, sometimes a day, sometimes a week or a month.

But the notice that stayed longest with me as a torment was a notice in a boot-mending shop in the High Street. Even to-day it sometimes creeps to the top of my mind and occupies the night watches. It was a printed card which said *There Is Nothing Like Well-Repaired Boots*. It trapped my attention the first time I saw it, and I never got away from it. I felt sure the man was not making that statement for the sake of making it, as one says It's a Fine Day or Twice Two are Four. There must, I felt, be some purpose behind it, some challenge ; and in all dreary hours, during algebra in class, or on Sunday mornings, or while my elders were gossiping, I would go round and round the statement, running through a mental catalogue of all the " things " I knew, hoping that I

might be able to prove him wrong, might some morning
be able to push open the door of his shop and shout
" There IS." But however much I thought and
thought, I was always in the end driven to admit
defeat and to grant that he was right. To this day I
cannot think of anything in the visible or invisible
world that in any way resembles Well-Repaired Boots.

Wherever there is conservatism there is " character,"
and our suburb bred many a character. Most of the
side-street shopkeepers were sharply flavoured with
" humours " of the Ben Jonson strain, and even some
of those in the more formal High Street. That boot-
mender must have been, since here he is, being remembered fifty years after his tantalising essay in
publicity. He was one of the few I didn't know. The
landlord of the big modern public-house was another ;
but you didn't need to know him ; to realise him you
had only to see him. Modern as his house was, he
himself seemed to have been drawn and coloured by
Cecil Aldin. He had a country face, a short white
beard and long white moustache, and wore a red
waistcoat, a gold albert chain four sizes larger than life,
a white hunting-stock, a gamekeeper's velveteen jacket,
riding breeches and a white bowler. In his buttonhole
he wore always a white carnation or gardenia, and in
his stock a diamond horseshoe pin that might have
been a nephew of the Crown Jewels.

One of the bakers was another. I don't think he
ever baked anything himself ; I was told, indeed, that
he knew nothing about it. But in the shop he always
wore a white smock and a chef's hat. I asked him
once when he did his baking, and he said " Ah." Then
I asked him why he wore the bakehouse costume when
he wasn't baking, and he said Putting ideas into
people's heads was half the battle in business. " Yes,
me boy, in business ye need to keep your eyes open."

" Why ? "

" Because if ye don't ye won't see anything." And
he gave a wise nod of the head, and one eyebrow went

up and the other went down, and I thought of our
Bank Holiday Fair on the Green and the switchback.

Almost every week he had a story for me, fantastic
or dramatic. The best of them was the story of the
five hundred jam-puffs. It became the best because
it never got itself told. He was always going to tell
it, and then a customer would come in, or he would
deliberately interrupt himself and dart away with a
promise to finish it to-morrow.

One story concerned a bakery kept by his grand-
father. The head baker was a small man, and one
night he was left alone in the bakehouse. He was
last seen standing at the long deep trough which held
the dough for the night's baking of the bread for the
whole of next day's customers. He was standing on
tip-toe, as he usually had to, and was bent double,
kneading the dough with his fists. Then (it was
supposed) his foot must have slipped behind him and
shot him forward head-first into the trough of dough.
That, anyway, was how they found him—hanging over
the trough, head and shoulders buried in the dough ;
suffocated ; dead. It was a tragic story but my
childish curiosity wanted to carry it a step farther,
even to anti-climax. There was a question I burned
to ask. But I was afraid. Three times I tried to ask
that question, and three times I checked myself. I
was afraid of what the answer might be. I was afraid
it would be such an answer that I would never again
be able to eat bread. So I never asked it. You can
guess what it was.

Another friend was the jeweller in the Crystal
Arcade. I don't know how I came to have his
acquaintance. Certainly not as a customer. But in
those days, though I made little acquaintance among
those of my own age, I readily made friends among my
elders. Later, when I was about nineteen, reserve set
in and has remained with me ever since. His window,
for its colour and lustre, was one of my daily delights,
and long and often as I stood before it I never exhausted

its interest. He was an elderly man with an elderly
scowl which loomed upon the world and its creatures
as noxious things for which he had no use. His
thunder dispersed only when he was handling his
jewels, which he handled as other men handle the
tresses of the beloved. The savage face then dissolved
into the sweetest of smiles and the true man was
revealed.

If no customers were present he always allowed me
to talk to him, and was always ready to show me the
various stones and answer my questions about them.
I would ask him, " What's that called ? " and " Where's
that come from ? " and he would roll out its name and
things about it as though pronouncing the Name
Unutterable. " That is an aquamarine. That is an
emerald. That is cornelian." Or it might be sardonyx
or topaz or amethyst ; or sapphire, beryl, jasper,
turquoise. Those names caught my ear with the
enchantment of a rune, and sometimes I would repeat
them to myself in bed as a sort of slumber-song. They
pointed for me the curious fitness with which men have
named certain lovely things—gems, colours, wild
flowers, and certain far-away rivers and hills. The
syllables are like a breeze, or the fall of the sea on
beaches ; sometimes storm and sometimes whisper.

Another friend was the old Italian with the hurdy-
gurdy on a pole, an instrument that must have been
new in the 'sixties, since its repertoire consisted solely
(though I didn't know that till later) of arias from
La Traviata, *Rigoletto* and *Un Ballo in Maschera*. I
knew only that those arias pleased my ear, and I made
the acquaintance of the grinder not by pennies which
I hadn't got, or by talk, but by standing and listening
with full attention. He seemed to appreciate this.
He would sometimes nod to me and smile and shake
his exotic ear-rings and say, " *Bella, bella, bella, no ?* "
Often he would make what appeared to be friendly
remarks, and I could make no response beyond an
awkward smile. Sometimes, when I had twice missed

his weekly recital, he would give me a mock bow when I did turn up, and say, " *Il fanciullino perduto.*" But it was he who became the lost one. He was found one morning, during the year of the Great Frost, sitting in a doorway, asleep for ever, with his head resting on the music-box of his beloved maestro Verdi.

Yet another friend was the keeper of the newspaper shop, where I sometimes spent one of my halfpennies on *Chips, Comic Cuts,* or the *Funny Wonder,* with the weekly adventures of Weary Willie and Tired Tim or Chokee Bill and Area Sneaker. In recognition of this custom he allowed me to look over the more adult comics—*Scraps, Snapshots, Ally Sloper, Nuggets, Pick-me-Up, Judy, Moonshine.* I found something in those comics which I couldn't define or even fully apprehend, but which made them for me much nearer to life than the records of the daily paper. Life *was* more like that than like the daily paper. The at-first-sight preposterous picture on the front page of *Ally Sloper* was a more true representation of a scene in many everyday homes than any newspaper report of similar matters. The very attitudes, extravagant as they were, were the attitudes of life. The scenes in those comics were scenes of life felt rather than seen ; they got beneath the defences of considered deportment ; and in looking at them I grasped, though without conscious understanding, the justification of caricature, and saw that it was always nearer to truth than the sober portrait.

The High Street, the broad and light and airy High Street in which the tallest shop was no more than two storeys, was much more my playground than the Green. Those characters made it my novel, a novel of unending chapters in which I could read of the magnetic mystery of life and of the many little worlds within this Chinese puzzle of a world. Every day it threw up something new to catch the fancy, some fresh aspect of the absorbing puzzle, and I could wander in it four or five

times a day, soaking up impressions like a piece of
blotting-paper.

I also made it the setting of many little games. One
of these, played when I was alone, was to read the
words on shop-fronts backwards and make queer people
and places of them. Thus, Saloon Bar became Rab
Noolas (from Scotland). Estate Agent became Tnega
Etatse (possibly an East African). Toys and Games
became Semag and Syot (music-hall comedians). Cigar
Divan became Navid Ragic (possibly from Iceland)
and Penny Bazaar was Raazab Ynnep (obviously a
Turk).

A game I often played with Freda was the Memory
game. Wherever there was a vacant site, or repairs
going on, there were hoardings bearing advertisement
posters. The game was to walk down the street, and
at the end to write down in exact order the goods
advertised, and then walk back and check our lists.
That game I always won. I could walk the whole
length of the street, and then recite, without one omission
or misplacement, a string of fifteen advertisements—
1. Nixey's Black Lead ; 2. Mother Siegel's Syrup ;
3. Vinolia Soap ; and then the Waterbury Keyless
Watch ; Montserrat Lime Juice ; Ridge's Food ;
Borax ; Dr. Williams's Pink Pills ; Liebig's Extract
of Meat ; Epps's Cocoa ; Horniman's Tea ; Hinde's
Curlers ; Geraudel's Pastilles ; HO for Breakfast ;
Sapolio. But in anything to do with figures Freda
always won, as in taking the number of a shop,
multiplying it by the number of people looking at it,
and seeing who could do it first ; or taking the figure
on the licence plate of a hansom and dividing it by the
hour of the day, or counting the number of articles in
the window of the big household store whose names
began with a certain letter.

The visual memory, such as I used on the posters, is
associated, they say, with a low order of intellect, and
there have been other indications of my standing far
from the first order. If the old legend is well founded

—that all the lofty successes in life were dunces at school—I suppose the converse is true. In my case it seems so since I always took each year three or four prizes—usually arid " improving " books—Trench on *The Parables*, Anne Pratt's *Wild Flowers*—that disguised their aridity by being bound in what the booksellers gorgeously call Full Crushed Crimson Levant Morocco Extra—which always suggests to me a mouthful of Victoria plums. Whatever form I was in, I usually took the History, the English Subjects, the French, the Geography and, unaccountably, the Religious Knowledge prize ; subjects requiring only memory. In mathematics I was always so low that often my papers were torn up. I could not understand even arithmetic, and as for algebra I still haven't any notion what those letters with figures over them are supposed to be up to ; or what situation could ever arise in my quiet life to make it necesary for me to prove that the angle at A was equal to the angle at B. I could not understand why they tried to stuff me with that useless wadding, or why they burdened our mathematical stars with the, to them, boring beauties of Spenser and Keats.

The history I was taught at school was not the history I wanted. It was not the history of England and its people. We were fed on Green's *Short History of the English People* : an excellent history of the *rulers* of England and their infantile intrigues, but a book that touches only slightly the subject of its title. The history of a nation's political life is not the history of that nation ; only the history of a very small but noisy and self-important department of that nation's life. All Histories of England were then of that kind, which meant that there was no real History of the English People until Traill's *Social England*, and we were never told about that. The Histories used in my childhood and youth gave us a lot of facts about kings and ministers and parliaments, and massacres and conquests on land and sea, but we were given no light on the real story of the English country and ourselves.

We were not taught why things were as they were in that present year ; how we came to be using the things we were using, how we came to be doing what we were doing, talking as we were talking, and living in the conditions in which we were living. We were not shown that things were as they were because of the continual change moving in nature and in the minds of men. We were not shown what the English people before us were doing and saying and using and eating at particular periods, which is the only real history. For all we knew the clothes we were wearing had just happened, and had been designed out of the air. We were never shown the continuity of our life, and how our clothes and furniture had developed, by gradual steps, from Saxon and Norman times. I had heard about fashions, but we were not shown that Fashion was not an arbitrary decree arising from the whims of tailors and dressmakers, but was, like folk-song, an expression of the contemporary spirit moving in the English people at a given time.

They taught us none of that. They taught us instead a great deal of falsehood which made propaganda for the established order by presenting crafty politicians as Great Men and single-minded rebels as rascals. It was implied that we were as happy and free as we were said to be because of the altruistic thought and labour of kings and their ministers. We were not told the truth ; that what was good in our life came from something greater than those figures ; from the spirit of the people of England operating through men whose names make no figure in the history books.

I found for myself far more English History in my High Street than ever I found in class, though I didn't then know it was history since the word had been corrupted for me. I had always a large appetite for the legend of things and of people. I found indeed more interest in a thing's legend than in the thing

itself. Most people are happy with facts and uncomfortable with truth, which has nothing to do with
facts, though the two are often confused. To be
offered the " truth " about something is almost always
to be offered a string of facts. But legend is far more
valuable than fact. The facts about a country are of
no help in understanding its people. To achieve that
you must study its legends. In them is preserved
the true spirit of a people, and in them you have the
clearest guide to national character. And my High
Street was thick with legends of the past, its signs
hanging from every door and window, influencing its
life and helping to make it what it then was. It was
charged with the spell of things gone and done with ;
a spell by which the most common things that are the
mere furniture of everyday, whether a meeting of
obscure lovers or the detail of trade or an old handbill
or the recovered transactions of a parish council,
become crystallised and set for ever as part of life's
poetry. The history of any High Street, indeed, would
be a much more reliable and luminous History of the
English People than any of those of the professional
and accepted historians ; and, though I did not then
understand this, I was sensible of it.

Besides being my novel and my history book the
High Street was an important factor in my private life
as the setting of certain rituals by which I ordered my
affairs. Like many children I cherished a number of
personal superstitions, some of them so absurd that I
kept them secret even from Freda. If I wanted some
pleasant thing to happen, or to escape some unpleasant
contingency, I went to school by way of the right-hand
side of the High Street instead of the left. If I wanted
fine weather for a certain day I would make a mental
vow that I would, in return, be specially sweet-
tempered for a week ; but the vow, to attain its
object, had to be made in the High Street. If made
elsewhere it was ineffective. On Saturday mornings,
wondering whether oranges would be three a penny or

four a penny, I convinced myself that if I went straight
to the High Street they would be three a penny, but
if I went by a roundabout cat-like route they would be
four a penny. If I stayed out late, I knew that if I
went home without passing through the High Street,
my staying out late would be noted and spoken about ;
if I went home via the High Street, even if it meant
going half a mile out of my way, nothing would be
said. If, when I went to see an aunt, I walked slowly
and sedately down the High Street, I was sure she
would give me a penny. If I ran I was sure she
wouldn't. All those protective observances, such is
the high puissance of faith, worked. On every occasion
the result was in accord with the procedure I had
observed or failed to observe. Even to-day I use one
or two secret and foolish magics of that kind, and they
invariably work.

CHAPTER IV

MAGIC AND MUSIC

ONE of the dissolving views that emerged from and
dissolved into that Kate Greenaway picture
was of a winter evening when I took Freda to the
Magic Lantern. I had talked and talked about it
until at last she gratified me by cutting one of her
practice-nights and joining me in that feast of colour.
For the appointed evening I made a special toilet. I
chose my " second-best " suit—a velvet sailor blouse
and knickers, with white singlet stamped with a blue
anchor and a bos'un's whistle strung round the neck
by a silvered lanyard. I spent five minutes over
cleaning my shoes, which had been twice cleaned that
day, and then I washed and then scrubbed my face
with a rough towel until it was sore, with the aim of
producing " roses." Then, for ten minutes, with

water and a hard brush, I " did " my hair. My hair was then brown and wavy, and I didn't like the waves ; I thought they looked soft and I liked to look smart. So I ruled and ruled those waves until I had ruled them into a flat brown plaster which, I was told by my mother, made me look like Soapy Sam. Then, with my Sunday cap and my only muffler, and an enamel button-portrait of Queen Victoria in the lapel of my blouse, I was ready.

The lantern shows were given in a small public hall, bleak and sterile as most public halls. It had three or four gas chandeliers with naked jets, a piano, and many rows of highly varnished and slightly sticky benches of pinewood. It had rafters of this pinewood and whitewashed walls. Its only wall decoration was three coloured charts showing the interior of a drunkard's stomach (black), the interior of a moderate drinker's stomach (brown) and a beautifully virgin splotch of rose-pink which was the precious stomach of the teetotaller. Two men, who went round certain of the neighbouring suburbs, giving one night a week to each, worked the shows, one at the lantern, and the other at the piano to supply incidental music and what would now be called a Running Commentary. The programme that evening was to open with *Hansel and Gretel*, to continue with *Three Blind Mice*, and to finish with *Scenes from the Life of Our Lord*. A very good pennyworth.

I waited for Freda at the Geneva Street end of the draughty passage, and we sauntered and lurched up the street to the hall. " It's funny," she said ; " I've done all sorts of things in my life but I've never once been to a Magic Lantern."

I said, " I hope you'll like it." Though she was going to pay her own penny, I was in the position of host, and I felt the responsibility and anxiety of a host. The evening might be a failure, and I would be sorry for her, ashamed of my own ineptitude in taking her to a failure, and ashamed of my admired Magic Lantern.

But she seemed prepared to enjoy anything, and we paid our pennies to the Patter Man, and crushed in with the others and scrambled for seats in the third row, and found gratification in the simple matter of sitting next to each other. I apologised for the decorations of the hall, but she said they would look better when the lights went down 'cos then we wouldn't be able to see them.

Then the Patter Man went to the piano and strummed a thundering chord, and the lights began to go down until there was only the feeblest glimmer, and the hall was a vault of shadow. And then there was the hushing of our babble, and the glare of the lantern on the white sheet, and the piano playing *Boys and Girls Come Out to Play,* and then the slow emergence of the first wonder of the evening—a glowing slide in red and blue and yellow of Hansel and Gretel at home in their parents' cottage—which was greeted by the usual approval of a long-drawn OO-oo-ooo. . . . We sat back and wallowed in colour, and above our heads the lantern sent through the dark a silver spear made of dancing dust.

The Patter Man began to read the story of Hansel and Gretel. He worked from a skeleton outline of material which gave him plenty of opportunity for improvising and gagging with topical and local allusions. We—the audience was all children—regarded him with respect and admiration as an advanced wit. The next slide showed the children in the wood, for which he played *Go to sleep, ma little piccaninny,* and in the patter he linked the wood with our Green. And then a slide that evoked quite a series of OO-oo-oo's and other exclamations—the slide of the witch's house made of almond-rock and chocolate and barley-sugar, and Hansel and Gretel breaking pieces from it. And then the slide which brought Oo's in a shriller key— the slide of the witch herself, with the piano giving, as appropriate music, *Her Golden Hair Was Hanging Down Her Back.*

As the show went on I could feel that Freda was suitably impressed, and my fears that I had over-painted the wonder of the Magic Lantern were stilled. Between the first and the second items she said she was glad she had come, and wouldn't have missed it for anything, and I felt so gratified that I almost believed I had invented Magic Lanterns and given the show myself. Sitting with her in that coloured darkness was a novel experience, and it gave me a novel and exquisite sensation. I discovered then that when you are sitting with people you can't see you are in much closer contact with their character, their personal aura. You come to know them through a sharper sense than the eyes. Freda and I were in closer companionship than we had ever been, and the sensation aroused by this made me shiver with new life, and made the pictures not just the coloured pictures they were when I went alone but something with a life of their own. They were part of me and part of Freda, and we were both somehow *in* them, moving in their scenes and washed in their colour.

In the first two items the Patter Man was able to let his acidulous wit run with some freedom in allusions to the keepers of local sweet-shops and the confectioners of the High Street, and to familiar street characters. The Three Blind Mice he impishly linked with the three partners of a well-known boot-store, and the farmer's wife with the head-mistress of the chief girls' school. But with the third item he made such a miraculous switch in voice and tone and manner that Freda could hardly believe he hadn't resigned the job to a substitute. The voice was as clerical as that of a new curate, and his cadences suggested that at the end of every sentence he was making his bow, and had never in his life made a joke. He had us far more hushed and still than the Vicar ever did, and with his approach to the Judas episode, and his dramatic pauses, and the hint of an impending emotional break-down, he had three children in tears—a great advance on the Vicar.

When it was all over, and we were tumbling out into the dark, Freda said it had all been lovely, especially the " dissolving " of one picture of blue and red and gold and the emergence from its ruin of another of green and white and violet. She said Daddy must get her a Magic Lantern for her birthday. Last birthday he had given her a stereoscope, which she had thought great fun, but of course the Magic Lantern was far better 'cos of the colours. " I can work the lantern. And you can make up stories about the pictures like the man did."

I shrank at that. " I don't think I could. You have to be very clever to make up things like he did all of a sudden."

" I don't suppose he did. I expect he's seen those slides before, and thought out what he was going to say."

" Perhaps so. He must be clever, though. The things he thinks of. That bit about the Home and Colonial Store." Just then he came out of the hall and passed in front of us. " Look," I said, " there he goes. Doesn't he look tired ? "

" It's trying work, I should think. Talking and making up those things and playing. Though the playing's easy. He was awfully solemn in the last pictures, wasn't he ? He must be very religious. But he does look tired."

He did. Or bored. He went straight across the road from the hall to the " Coach and Horses," and pushed open the lighted door with his foot, and we heard him shout, " Wotcher, George ! Here's yer old Thursday Reg'lar. And what a thirst ! "

On the way home I asked her when she was going to let me hear her play. I had constantly pressed her to give me that treat, but she had always put me off with excuses that her playing was nothing and she couldn't think why I wanted to hear her. But this time she gave in and said if I really wanted to, what about Sunday afternoon ? I could go along with her then to her practice on her Aunt's superior piano. So we fixed that I would call for her, and we parted in the draughty passage, and she said she had had a lovely evening, and wished they held them on some other evening than Thursday so's we could go together every week, and we stood simmering, and then abruptly ran away from each other.

People would have said that we two children had been to a Magic Lantern show. We had. And the magic of that hour of sitting with Freda in the dark was so strong that it has stayed with me all these years.

.   .   .   .   .

On my visits to Freda's home I always noted a particular difference between hers and mine. It wasn't only that they had more money, and had a house where we had only lodgings, and better furniture and more " things." It was the difference between a home that had a Father and a home that hadn't. Homes with Fathers in them seemed to me more furnished. Where there was a Father there was always something going on. A Father, I felt, made all the difference between a cosy little place where you lived and a real Home. My father had died in my first year.

Freda's home was real enough, with that reality which, when first encountered, seems like the creation of a disordered fancy. There are hundreds of homes of that kind in London, as solid and actual as anything can be on this whirling star, yet belonging far more to mad legend than to a world of ratepayers. In the side-streets of our suburbs all sorts of purple lives are living and one street of a hundred houses can hold not only a hundred different lives, but lives lived in a hundred different worlds. People live next door to each other, and might be living on different stars, so incongruous are their material and mental experience and points of view. They use the same kind of things, yet see them and use them in wholly different ways.

They use the same words and mean violently different
sentiments.   Their paths in London never cross ; they
never visit the same houses or meet in the same public
places ; their interests never converge, and they even
see the street they live in as a street that, if they
described it, would be unrecognisable by their neigh-
bours.   Officialism never realises this.   It talks of the
Public, and legislates for the Public, as though the
Public were one standard creature living in one uniform
world with one uniform conception of a world.   It
seems incapable of understanding that at any time
forty million people are living in forty million different
worlds, into which nothing of the other conceptions
of a world would fit.

I first saw Freda's home one Sunday morning.   I
was calling to take her to church, or she was taking
me.   On Sundays her father and her elder sisters and
brother were free of the week's workaday restrictions,
and, mad as the house was at other times, that freedom
turned it into something out of pandemonium.   That
atmosphere of pandemonium was intensified by the
roaring efforts of her father to reduce it.   The family
of six contrived somehow to give the illusion that they
were sixty.   You would have thought you were in a
country-house party where there were neither the
servants nor the space and conveniences of a country-
house.   They all got up at different hours—or didn't
get up.   Some wanted one kind of breakfast and some
another ; one wanted breakfast in bed and didn't get
it ; another wanted no breakfast and got it.   The
bedrooms, of which I had a sight, looked as though
they had been visited by an exasperated burglar.
Nothing in the house seemed to be in place.   One saw
underclothes on the stairs, hats in the dining-room,
cleaned silver on the umbrella-stand, tea-trays on the
hall table, overcoats on the landing.

Voices rang or shrilled in accusation of taking a
camera, borrowing a tennis-racket, stealing cigarettes ;
and all cried for the one maid Molly.   In spite of their

getting up at different hours, some twist of chance and probabilities made it impossible for any one of them to find the bathroom free. There were piteous and furious appeal, and tart and flinty refusal to be hurried. From different parts of the house came noises that made one think that four or five cats were dashing about tied to the crockery and fire-irons ; and above all that din came the howling objurgation of the head of the house from downstairs or from his bedroom— " For God's *sake*, can't we have a bit of peace in this house ? "

The repeated cries for Molly never produced her. The name Molly hints at youth, open eyes, yellow hair. Molly of Lamorna Road was around sixty, and had the face of the least agreeable of the Three Witches. She could hardly have heard of Zen Buddhism, but she had advanced far in its principles and practice. She seemed to know that the easiest way of satisfying a want is to ignore it ; that the best way of seeing a thing is to look away from it ; that the sure way of answering an appeal is not to hear it ; that the most effectual way of doing a thing is to do something else ; that the firmest logic is the inconsequential. Still moving in Zen, she contrived, with her tight grey hair, beady eyes and stony mouth, still to be a Molly. She had been devoted to the family, I learned, for twenty-four years. Her devotion was one of their burdens. She bullied all of them ; all except Freda's mother. To her she gave that patronising and amused tenderness that one gives to the weak, the infantile and the afflicted.

I cannot recall the appearance of the mother. She was there—that was all. She was always there, and had so permanently been there that the family seemed to regard her as a fixture, like the dining-room sideboard, and gave her little more attention than they gave it. Her laugh I do recall because I only twice heard her laugh. It was like the neigh of a funeral horse. And I did notice the high-powered scent she used. It was a crescendo of *mille-fleurs* to the point of eight or nine thousand.

Daddy, so Freda had told me, was in the Department of something or other at Whitehall, but she didn't know what he did there except that it must be something very trying because it gave him such a temper. On Sundays the family got the full blast of that temper, and it was so fierce and sustained throughout the day that Freda's elder sister once told me, in his presence, that there couldn't be any more bad temper in London ; His Lordship had got it all. Not that anybody was upset by it. They ignored it and him as they ignored their mother, except when they wanted something.

Some mature bachelors have all the air of being fathers of families, and some fathers of families have the air of being bachelors. Freda's father was one of those. His wife looked like the mother of several children, but he looked like the eldest of his own, though without the authority of an eldest. When he was not in a temper he wavered and wandered about the house as though looking for something and unable to think what it was. If people expressed surprise that so young-looking a man should be the father of four children, two of them grown up, he would say that some men grew signs of age by letting family cares weigh upon them. He never did. Children could sometimes be a bit of a handful, but they only needed system and a firm but tactful control—using an inflated phrase for a performance he had never given.

On the appointed Sunday afternoon I called for Freda, and, after a number of false starts and dishevelled explanations to three different members of the family of where she was going and for what, she managed to wriggle out of the maelstrom of 24 Lamorna Road, and we went across the Monkeys' Parade, which the High Street became on Sunday afternoons and evenings, and across the Green and up to the Grove. On the way she told me about her Aunt.

" Auntie's a Soprano." I didn't know what that

was, so I kept quiet. "She gets awfully good notices in the papers. She doesn't think much of Mummy. They never got on together when they were young. She calls Mummy a Piece of Wet Fish. And she calls Daddy the Flattened Doughnut. You mustn't tell anybody, though. They don't know she calls them that."

"She's rather rude, isn't she?"

"Oh, she is. She's rude to everybody. But they don't take any notice like they would if it was other people. She's got that sort of way with her. She gives everybody a nickname. Mr. Hemstrode the Vicar, you know—she calls him the Death Rattle. And my brother Carlo she calls the Emetic."

"What's an emetic?"

"I don't know. But that's what she calls him. She calls me the Face-ache."

I was indignant. "Whatever for?"

"Don't know. Anyway, I don't mind."

For the moment I was prejudiced against the Aunt. I wondered what name she would find for me if she honoured me with that much notice, and I hoped I wouldn't see her. I felt I wouldn't like her.

The house was a late Georgian house, or perhaps cottage *ornée* of that period, with a large garden all round it—flower-garden, kitchen-garden, orchard, shrubbery, rosery—and a huge front lawn guarded by a cedar. On the front door was a card printed in large type—OUT. BACK AT 6.0. I was glad to know that I wouldn't see her, though I wondered why she didn't leave it to the servants to tell people she was out. Then I wondered whether it was the servants' day out, and if so how we would be able to get in. But Freda rang the bell, and the door was opened by a parlour-maid who was as sharp a study in black-and-white as a wood-cut. She wore a dead-black dress, a fiercely white bib-apron and collar, and a white linen cap with two broad white streamers floating from it down to the waist. She looked at us as though saying,

E

" I have to open the door to you brats, but how dare you disturb me ! " But she let us in.

The house inside was all cool and dainty and soft, and the chief colours were yellow and old-gold. Living there, I felt, must be like living inside a daffodil. Just as we got in, the Aunt, to my surprise, came in from the garden, and I was presented, and my prejudice was blown away. There was no question of liking or disliking. I was aware only of awe. By her height, her erect bearing, her voluminous old-gold gown, her piled hair, her three-inch ear-rings and her imperious eyes, she was the exact opposite of her sister, and she looked to me so much more like the Queen of England than the good and stout Victoria that I almost knelt. In a high voice she said, " Hullo, Face-ache," and gave her a smile as frigid as diamonds. After half a look at me which didn't seem to see me, and without any word as to who I was, she waved us to a door at the end of a long passage, and told Freda to go on in, and for God's sake to shut *both* doors.

As we went down the passage I said to Freda, " She's at home, then. Why does she say she's Out ? "

" Well, she *was* out. Out in the garden. She doesn't like seeing people Sunday afternoons."

" I see. And at six o'clock she's ready to see them."

" No. At six o'clock she *really* goes out."

I pondered that. " That sounds funny."

" Well, she *is* funny, at times. Often I don't understand her at all. I asked her the other day whether Liszt was supposed to be a better composer than Mendelssohn, or whether Mendelssohn was better than Liszt, and all she said was that she liked Clapham Junction better than either of them."

" What do you think she meant ? "

" Don't know at all. I take no notice when she talks like that."

The room at the end of the passage had an ordinary door and behind it a baize-covered door, to both of which Freda attended. It looked on to part of the

garden—the rosery—and it had nothing in it but two
sofas, a few chairs, and the long, sleek, gleaming body
of a piano. "It's an Erard," Freda said, but she
might as well have said it was a brontosaurus. I
thought pianos were just pianos, and that the only
difference was that some were Grand and some were
ordinary.

After pointing out bits of the garden to me, she
strolled and lurched over to the shining black monster,
and seated herself at it without apparently being the
least afraid of it, and became a white dot attached to
its surface. From where I was told to sit I could just
see the top half of her head. Far from being afraid
of it, she seemed to treat it as something quite tame
that had got to do what she told it. She strummed a
bit, just, I thought, to show it that she didn't care, and
then began to play.

I had wanted to hear her play, but after it was done
I wished I hadn't. I felt I wouldn't be able to treat
her any more as an easy everyday friend. Her playing,
which no doubt was as crude as any girl's of her age,
and as Awful as she said it was, to me, ignorant as I
was, was a revelation. I had been impressed by her
accompanying at the Singing Class, but this was something far beyond that. It made me a little afraid of
her. The girl whose small hands were producing from
that monster that thunder and ripple and peal was
somebody I didn't know. It seemed to set her far
away. I was sorry. But how I was thrilled.

When the first piece was done she sat still and looked
at me across the length of the piano, and giggled.
She said it was one of Schumann's Noveletten, which
conveyed nothing to me. I knew no music save that
of the street-organ, and all I could think of what she
had played was that it was Wonderful. She went on
playing—four, five, six different pieces, and I sat and
marvelled. She told me she was playing Mozart,
Mendelssohn, Chopin, Brahms. I only knew that she
was playing me silly. I suppose that all I had heard

was just a suburban child's strumming. Perhaps.
But it made the room and the garden and the world
unfold. The colours in the room and the garden were
sharper ; the scent of the late flowers coming through
the french window was keener ; Freda herself was
dressed with a new significance, and so was I. All the
factors of my life were brought together by that music,
and fused into one warm glow—my home, my school,
the High Street, the Green, the long shining summer
of that year, the stories I was reading—all flooded into
that room and impinged upon Freda and the piano ;
and once again I was living in real life. The mystery
of everything was still a mystery, but the music made
it a luminous, not a dark mystery.

After a long silence following her last piece I said,
" I don't know anything about it, but you *are* a good
player, aren't you ? "

She said, " No, I don't think so. Nobody's ever
said so. Just ordinary."

" But other girls who play don't play like you, do
they ? "

" Most of 'em never trouble to learn. And don't
practise. You see, I've been playing for years and
years. Ever since I can remember. Perhaps that
makes a difference. But you wait till you hear somebody *really* play. You'll know then."

I sauntered home to tea with her, and on the way,
still in a daze, I thought about what I had heard and
what seemed to me the marvel of it, and then I asked
her, " What *is* music ? "

" How do you mean ? D'you mean how you tell
good music from silly stuff ? "

" No. I mean what is it itself ? What is it to
begin with ? It isn't in those black dots on the page.
It isn't in the keys of the piano. It isn't in the wires
at the back. It isn't in your fingers. And yet it
happens out of all those things. What is it itself ? "

We were on the Green, and she stopped, and leaned
against a tree and stood on one leg with puckers all

over her face. Then, with a sudden clearing, she said,
" Well . . . first of all, of course, somebody thinks it
in his head. The composer, before he writes it down,
thinks it and hears it."

" But how does he begin thinking it ? "

" Mmmm . . . I don't know. But that must be
what happens. Yes. It's thought. Only thinking
in sounds instead of words, and then talking in sound.
Music's just another way of talking. And it goes
through all those things—paper, fingers, keys, wires—
to get to us. But first of all it's the composer's
thought."

" But where does he get the thought from ? "

" Goodness knows. Perhaps it comes out of some
Thought-place in the sky, like lightning. And strikes
one person out of millions. Like lightning does. It's
a mystery."

I agreed that it was, and I spent the rest of the
afternoon and evening in worrying about it.

.   .   .   .   .

It was a week or so later that she gave me my first
experience of real music with a real orchestra and a
real pianist. Her Aunt, who had tickets for everything, had tickets for an Albert Hall concert. She
couldn't take Freda herself, as she often did for
education, so the elder sister took her, and as there
was a third ticket Freda asked that I might go with
them because she wanted me to hear what the piano
was when it was really played, which would show me
how any other playing was nothing.

It didn't do that, but it did take me into a world of
even greater mystery. Before the concert began she
tried to explain to me the different items, so far as her
musical knowledge went, but I was too bewildered in
watching the assembling of the great orchestra to pay
much attention, and none of it meant anything to me.

When the concert did begin I was aware only of the
presence of real life in a new form. I was aware only

of Sound, of a soaring and falling and surging sea of
Sound. And all that Sound seemed to hover above
the orchestra like a presence summoned by the conductor's wand, which of course it was. It brought to
my mind a Bible phrase—" Behold I show you a
Mystery." And indeed I was taking part in something
that was both a Mystery and a mystery. Yet while
it was a vast volume of Sound it seemed to my fancy
to be born of its opposite ; it seemed to come from a
core of Silence and to return again to Silence ; and I
found myself puzzling again on what music *was*, and
wondering whether it wasn't, after all, only the voice
of Silence. But all my attention was held by that
sea and rain of Sound ; rain of gold and silver, and
sea of violet or green, and pianissimo passages for
strings that were the very sleep of Sound. I heard
that flood of Sound with more than ears and mind ;
my skin heard it and my eyes and hair. Silver rain
was falling ; rain that glittered and rang ; and the
horns shot it with gold, and the flutes were flashes of
white light, and the 'cellos were brown clouds, and the
harp was blue like frozen ponds under moonlight.

I had no notion that in thus letting my fancy play
I was committing a musical sin. But when, during
the break between two items, I tried to say something
of it to Freda I was, with a gentle but perceptible sniff,
reproved. None of those fancies, she said, had anything to do with music. She understood how I got
them, but speaking as a musician I shouldn't have had
them. It showed I wasn't really paying attention to
the music itself. When I knew more of music I would
grow out of it. I must pay proper attention to the
Concerto, and not go off mooning.

I tried to follow her command, but it was hopeless.
She whispered to me about the technical excellences
of the pianist, and what he did and what he didn't ;
and it was all nothing to me. I was drowned in the
silver thunder that came from the piano, and incapable
of taking in anything she said. I was drowned and

drunk with Sound, more drunk than any alcohol in later years could make me ; and finally she gave it up and left me to my ineptitude and ignorance.

We agreed in later talks that whatever I might make I would never make a musician : I hadn't got even the elements of it. But I had met the presence and the power of Sound, and if I couldn't listen intelligently to an orchestra, I could go with the composer so far as attaining through Sound to a fuller consciousness of a thousand new points and facets of life and of the human soul.

CHAPTER V

SWEET LAVENDER

IN my long friendship with Freda—long, because three years to a child has the duration of an adult's thirty—there were occasions of which every detail remains with me, and other occasions, at the time more weighty, of which nothing survives. One of the trivial and transitory occasions that remains in high relief was the Lavender occasion, perhaps because it was an episode of Crime and Punishment in which we both suffered, and because it showed me that those juvenile Moralities, the religious novelettes and tracts at which I had always scoffed, were not so far out as I had thought in their fables of Retribution.

It happened on a Saturday of late summer, when the street-organs were tiring everybody's ears with the air of *Dorothy Dean*. We met in the High Street, Freda in a mauve silk frock, with white silk sash and floppy black straw hat ; myself in white sailor blouse and knickers ; both of us wearing thin sand-shoes. Neither had a programme for the day, so we strolled up to the Green, and then walked and walked. Right across the length of the Green we went, to its very end, and

then we came out to the main road, and followed that
until we reached a point where the tram-lines ended.
Beyond that I had never been, but Freda said, " Let's
walk on, shall we, and see what we find ? " So we
did. We went on southward into far and foreign
countries.

For a time the main road was nothing but large and
lofty houses set back behind laurel bushes, and there
was little to interest us. It was a warm grey day, with
no life in the sky or air, and therefore no life in human
veins or in the streets or in the shapes of the houses
or their windows. Faces were apathetic. Movements
were listless. Tradesmen's carts and tricycles crawled.
Everything seemed to have been arrested in a half-
doze. We too were in it, and walked like the others,
without any of our usual stir and response to everything
we saw. I was going to say to her, " This is dull.
Let's turn back," when the main road began to go
downhill, and looking to the bottom of the hill we saw
a line of shops and some whirl of people. That was a
New Place to both of us, and when she said, " Let's
just go down and see what it's like, and if there's no
fun we'll come back," I said, " All right."

So we went down, and we found that there were a
few points of interest. The shops were different.
They were not our shops ; they belonged to aliens of
another suburb, and their windows held unfamiliar
things and were dressed in a new way, and the shoppers'
faces were new faces. So there was something to
observe and remark upon, and we went from shop to
shop, from one side of the road to the other, until we
came to the end of them. And then we saw a long
line of little houses with neat front gardens, much
larger than our own, and then a railway-station, and
then some more shops. So we went on. We had not
spent our Saturday money, and Freda thought it would
be exciting to spend it in a New Place, and I agreed,
and we decided to spend it at the first nice shops we
came to.

We found two or three nice shops, and after some discussion she bought out of her sixpence an ice-cream for each of us, and I, having only a penny, bought two pears at a halfpenny each. As we walked on we tried to discover which went better after which, and agreed that she would eat ice-cream first and follow it with a pear, and I would follow pear with ice-cream. When this was done, we considered each other's report, and decided that either way was a mistake, and that pears and ice-cream were not made for each other.

We tried to learn the name of the New Place, but could see nowhere any sign. Then, at a cross-road, we saw a bus setting off into the sideroad. She wanted to know where it was going, but we were too far from it to see anything except that it was green. " Looks nice along that road," she said. " Let's see where it goes to. It must go *somewhere* or it wouldn't have a bus." I agreed that as the bus was going that way it was pretty certain that somewhere down the road was a place where people of some sort lived—eccentric people, no doubt ; and she said, " Well, let's see what it's like. We've got plenty of time, and it's rather fun seeing places where you don't live yourself. They look funny, some of them, don't they ? You'd hardly think people would want to live in them. I remember going with Daddy to a place called St. John's Wood. It isn't a bit like our side of London. The High Street's quite different. Doesn't look like a High Street. And another place I went to when I was quite young. Called Shepherd's Bush. Silly name, isn't it ? It hasn't got a High Street at all. Fancy a place not having a High Street."

I agreed that it was queer, and said there were lots of queer places in London. " I've been to one or two, but I don't know just where they are, or whether I could find them again. Some places look so queer you can hardly believe people get used to them. A place I saw at night—place called Islington—it didn't

seem a bit like London. It's on a hill, and you look
down on all sorts of things—big stations and churches
and enormous buildings, and miles and miles of roofs
of houses. It didn't seem real to me. I felt as though
I'd got out of my own life into somebody else's. You
know what I mean ? ''

  " Yes. I know. I've had that feeling too. Like
when you see a town from a railway—as I sometimes
have when we've been going to the seaside. They
seem like something out of a book, and the people in
the street don't look like real people—they look like
clockwork things going in and out of the shops, don't
they ? It's as though you're looking over the edge of
the world into another world. I often wonder, looking
down at those places, what it'd feel like to live in them.
You think it must feel quite different and be quite a
different life from your own place. But perhaps after
all it isn't. Perhaps all places are ordinary when you
get to know them. I don't know, though. Once,
coming back from the country after dark, the train
went across a bridge, and I looked down into a street
all lights and shops, and people going in and out,
fearfully exciting, and there were two girls going into
a cake shop. I just got a sight of them as the train
went across, and they looked so nice—I *did* want to
know them and go and stay with them. And all the
way home I wondered what sort of life they had in
that town, and where they went to school, and what it
was like, and what they did on holidays. That street
of shops looked so wonderful, and everybody looked as
though they enjoyed living there, that I felt sure it
must be much jollier living there than where we are.
But I'll never see it again, and I'll never see those
girls as long as I live, 'cos I don't know what place it
was. I asked Daddy what it was, and he didn't know
either. I only know it was on the London and South
Western Railway. Though sometimes I feel that
perhaps it wasn't there. That perhaps I didn't see it
—that I went to sleep in the train and just dreamt it.

I don't know. But it's—— Oh, look—isn't that nice ? "

We had come to a point on the road taken by the bus where it opened out into a sort of square, with a line of flower-beds in the middle. There were shops and houses on each side of the square, and roads leading off each side, and buses going this way and that, and in the middle of the flower-beds was a large and brand-new clock-tower with a notice saying it was erected by Public Subscription to commemorate something or other of local importance.

We stood and stared about the place, as though it were the scene of a play, and something exciting, like an Opening Chorus, was about to happen. Nothing did happen. The strange buses arrived and went ; the strange people hovered about the shops ; the strange shopkeepers came out to the doors to speak to them, and the strange clock-tower stood new and unregarded. That was all. Then Freda said, " I don't know in the least where we are. Do you ? " I said, " No. It's all quite new to me. I never knew there was such a place." " Come on," she said ; " let's have a good look round while we're here."

So we did. When, as a child, you see a place for the first time, you see it as it is ; you take it, as it were, by surprise, when it is being itself and not affected by your gaze and accommodating itself to your eyes. Seeing each new place is like being born again into a new life, with virgin eyes and virgin mind. Repeated visits never again reveal its true form and spirit. It is the first sight only that does that, so that each new place is, in more senses than one, a strange place. I have since passed many times through that little suburb, but never again have I seen it as I saw it then —as it is, magical, something that people, if they could *see*, would go out to see as they go out to see the little towns of Europe.

We walked once round the square. Then she pointed down one of the roads and said, " It looks interesting

down there. Let's just go down it, shall we ? " So
we did. I didn't know how far we had walked by
then, and I didn't know whether I was tired or not,
and didn't ask whether she was. The interest of the
occasion over-rode anything of that sort. It was a
street of villas of a style different from those of our own
suburb, and with different flowers in the front gardens
and different lamp-posts. Some of the flowers were
quite new to me, but Freda, having a garden, was able
to tell me their names, though as most of them were
of three or four syllables I forgot them a minute after.

As we went on and on, the houses became thinner,
and the road made a bend. We followed the bend,
and then Freda said, " Look ! I do believe we're
getting into the country."

I said, " I believe we are. It looks all open."

" It does. Isn't it exciting ! "

If it wasn't the country, it was certainly the end of
that suburb, and one of the world's great open spaces.
We could see no more buildings ; nothing but horizon
with a smudge that might have been hills. On our
right was a lane with hedges and trees, which my
knowledge of the trees on our Green enabled me to
identify as elms. " Let's go down here," she said,
" then we'd better turn back. I wonder what the
time is. We might see a rabbit."

We went down the lane, prying here and there,
until, at a turn, we saw something that brought us
both to a stop. Freda exclaimed, " Whatever's that ?
Why, I do believe it's—— It looks like—— But it
can't be. It looks like—like the sea. But it can't be,
can it ? " I didn't know, but I felt it couldn't be.
I didn't think we had come as far as that. Though
certainly it was a phenomenon I hadn't met before.
A long footpath leading from the lane opened on to an
immense and unending sheet of what, if it wasn't sea,
was blue smoke.

" I know," I said. " The field's on fire, and it's
smouldering."

" Let's go and see. Come on."

So we ran down the long footpath, and then broke into the open, and came upon the sea or smouldering field. And there she threw back her head and sniffed and sniffed, and then broke into laughter, and said one word—" Lavender ! " Before us stretched field after field, acre after acre, of lavender, whose name is like its perfume, stealing out of itself and dying in the moment of birth. Nothing but lavender and lavender. The grey air was drowsy with it, as the prospect was blue with it. It came right up to the edge of the footpath, and there were clusters of it growing even in the path itself. There were such masses of it, and it looked and smelt so clean and fresh, that I felt it would look just right in Freda's white sash or her hat, and that there would be no harm in picking a few of the stalks from the footpath.

So I picked a few stalks, and Freda, seeing what I was at, picked some too, and said it was lovely stuff to put with your handkerchiefs, and we went on picking, and she said her grandmother used to have lavender-bags in every box and drawer and——

And then came earthquake and chaos. From behind a hedge came a huge air-filling roar that made us both jump backwards, and out of the hedge burst the biggest man I had ever seen, with the blackest of all black beards, holding above his head the largest stick in the world. I jerked Freda by the arm, and she turned, and I turned. We dropped our stalks of lavender. In a high squeal she cried, " Run. He's after us. Run ! " And she ran, and I ran, and the man ran. Behind us he roared, and we heard the thud of his boots. But Freda could run like a cat, and I was almost as swift. We tore down that footpath in a matter of seconds. As we went I heard a jingle of something on the stony path, but nothing just then was of importance except getting away.

Out of the footpath into the lane. Up the lane, legs going like cabwheels. Out of the lane into the road of

villas. I was dashing into that road when Freda
cried, " No—not that way. Look—the Man's not
behind us. He's gone over the field to cut us off.
He'll be waiting there. Go straight on." That came
out in gasps. She shot across the road, and I followed.
We were in another road of villas, and I trusted to her
sense to know which way to go. We panted side by
side, not now at a sprint but at a jog-trot. She said,
" If—we—go on—we can—turn at—the end. And
get back—that way—to the—clock-tower."

We ran in fear. Little thrills of cold chased little
thrills of hot up and down my back. But in the very
intensity of the fear I knew that that was one of the
hours when I had got into real life. I was on the edge
of disaster, and I learned to my surprise that it was a
rapturous state to be in. We ran on and on, and
somewhere we turned left when we should have turned
right, and got into a long half-built road with no turning. There was nothing to do, with the menace of the
Man behind us, but to follow it to its end. So we
jogged on.

And then came the rain. It didn't announce its
coming by the usual preliminary spits or trial shower.
It came. All at once. With everything it had. In
one continuous sheet that was like a fog. Our jog-trot
slowed. Freda looked at me with blank eyes. I
dropped to a walk and looked right and left for shelter.
There was none. Only low hedges and open fields
with not a single tree. And if there had been shelter
we couldn't have used it. There was the Man. We
could only go on.

We were breathless, with tight chests, and already
half-drowned. The rain was dancing on and pouring
off her floppy hat, and beating its limp brim even
limper, and my cap was as sodden as though it had
lain in a pond. I could feel wet on my shoulders and
knees ; my sand-shoes were puddles. Her frock was
shining but no longer with silkiness. One of her
garters had snapped in the run, and the sodden stocking

kept slipping down. After two or three tugs she let
it go, and squelched on with one bare leg and one
stockinged leg. And the spiteful rain came faster,
stinging the face like drops of wet fire, and the road
came to an end, and there was a wide brook and no
way out.

We said nothing. We turned and squelched back.
When we got to where we had entered it she said,
" D'you think we—dare go—that way ? To the place
where—the buses are ? "

I said, " I shouldn't think—he's waiting—there.
Not in—the rain. Let's—chance it."

" We'd better—run then. And get the next—bus
—case they only—run now and—then. I've got—
fourpence and—it'll take us—part of the—way to—
where we first—saw it. Can you—still run ? "

I nodded and we made a dash for it, throwing glances
right and left and behind. But there was no Man.
There was only the rain, hissing at our futile attempts
to escape it. Not a single person was in the streets,
and when we came to a point where we picked up our
original trail at the end of the lane, there was no sign
of life anywhere. We jogged on, steaming in a cloud
of wet and misery. Freda jerked out, " Wonder—how
often the—buses run." And she stopped and screamed.

The scream was so sharp that I thought at first that
the Man had become invisible and had clutched her
with an unseen hand. But she didn't look as though
it was that. She was staring straight ahead, with
white eyes, and her hand was at her sash. " What's
the matter ? " I said. " You ill ? "

She looked at me out of a streaming face. Rain was
streaming from all points of her and from all points of
myself. Her black hair hung in ropes. " My money ! "
It was a wail.

" What about it ? "

" It's gone. I've lost it. Every penny."

" But how—— ? " Then I remembered the jingle
on the stones and told her.

In the tones of death she said, " Then we can't have
a bus. We can't go back and look for it. We daren't
—that Man. We'll have to walk—walk all the way
home—like this. All the way."

We stood like sponges with the resolution of sponges.
Then I said, " Well, if we must, we must. Perhaps
the rain'll stop soon. It does sometimes when it comes
on suddenly. We must just push on."

She hunched up her sodden shoulders, and we went
on. So did the rain. She began to wail. " Oh dear
—I wish we hadn't come. I wish we'd never touched
that lavender. Then I wouldn't have lost the fourpence. And we could have had the bus. I'm so
tired."

I could think of nothing to say except, " Cheer up.
We've got to go on. There's nothing else we can do.
I'm sorry."

" I wonder how far we've come."

" I never noticed."

" No. We've come too far. We ought to have
thought. I wonder what time it is. It feels late.
Like afternoon."

" I expect it is."

She gave another wail. " O-oh—the rain's pouring
all down my neck."

" Well, take your hat off. That's where it's coming
from. It'll be better without it. I'm not wearing my
cap. It's soaked."

She took it off, and a shower fell from it right in my
face. We squelched forward, and turned a corner,
and came into the road where we had first struck the
" country," and at the end we could see the square and
the clock-tower and the buses. It seemed a long way,
but at last we reached it, and found the road by which
we had come, and the cross-road, and we went on and
on to the cross-road, and on again into the main road,
until it seemed that we had never been doing anything
at all except plodding, soaked and spat on, with one
dead leg moving before the other. And as we plodded

my feet went to the air of a comic song, current at that
time, which had ridiculously come to my mind, and
was going round and round in senseless repetition—
It ain't all lavender. . . .

And then the rain stopped.

And then came thirst. The hot and thundery day
and the breathless run and the long plod had induced a
thirst such as I had never known. I wasn't legs and
arms and head. I was Thirst—an aching lust of mouth
and throat, and nothing in sight or prospect to give
me ease. It was forbidden to me ever to drink from
public drinking-fountains, but if I could anywhere
have seen one that prohibition would have been forgotten. I would have drunk from anything. I even
wished I could see a cart of Carlo Gatti & Stevenson,
so that I might, as street-boys did, sneak a fragment
of ice from its tail-board. I thought of that piece of
ice sluicing about my mouth, and the thought was as
tormenting as the thirst. It induced other thoughts.
Thoughts of a long glass of ginger-beer with ice-cream
in it—ginger-beer-and-ice-cream with its crisp white
foam. I could feel its impact on the palate and the
ripple and gush of its frozen whiteness along the aching
throat. Thoughts of iced lemon-squash ; of glasses
of sharp lime-juice ; of the cool tang of Mason's Herb
Beer which I had first tasted that summer ; thoughts
of a long draught of hot tea, of a dewy slice of melon ;
thoughts of glasses of anything, even milk, no favourite
of mine—six of them all in a row, one after the other
going cold and tingling to the relief of my personal
desert. I said nothing to Freda. I was afraid she
might be suffering too, and to talk about it would only
make it worse. So we plodded on.

And then, lifting my head, I saw that we had come
out at the railway-station at the bottom of the hill,
and the second line of shops where we had had our
ice-cream. And I said, " Look, Freda. There's the
station. Cheer up. We'll be home in another hour."

She gave a little high yell. " What ! Another

F

hour ! " She stopped and lurched against a wall, and stood leaning on it with head bowed. Dead-tired as I was, I watched her with alarm, fearing she was going to fall. But she didn't. With a jerk she lifted her head, and shocked my own exhaustion right out of me. For the first time I saw her serenity shattered. Freda, the gentle Freda, let out a burst of words that she could only have got from her Aunt. " Oh—my—God. I'm so bloody tired I can't go another damn-bloody step ! "

The shock to me was so sharp that I stepped back, and my foot slipped off the kerb, and went into a six-inch puddle of mud. I said, " *Freda !* " in a tone of astonishment, dismay, alarm, sympathy, reproach and sorrow. She didn't look up. Her head was hanging at right angles to her shoulder, and she muttered, " Don't care. I'll say it again. And worse."

I realised that I shouldn't have spoken of another hour. If I had said nothing we would have gone plodding on, and she would not have collapsed. And now here she was, soaked to the skin, like myself, and apparently immovable. I myself was so upset by our plight, and my temper was so much on edge, that I was already at the point of being prepared to quarrel with her about anything. Her collapse sharpened the edge, and I was ready then to flare up with bitter words and say, " It's all your fault that we're like this. If you hadn't kept saying, Let's go on, we wouldn't be here." But luckily I realised that I wanted to quarrel, so I determined that I wouldn't let it happen. But for a moment or so I hated her, and was blaming her for everything, including the rain.

In that spasm of self-control I went up to her and said, all husky, " I'm sorry, Freda. I know how you feel. But it isn't *very* far now. We know where we are. And it isn't raining. We've got to do it some-how, and we can do it slowly. I can do it if you can. I couldn't do it alone. If you can't do it I shall lie down here and go to sleep."

At that she looked up. And then, with an air of having thought of something, she jerked herself away from the wall, and cried, " Why, of *course*. What a selfish beast I am. Of course, you're as tired as I am. And I was only thinking of myself. I *am* mean."

I said quickly, " Of course you're not. You're only tired."

" Yes, I am mean. And I'm sorry." Then, with the inconsistency of the female, on the point of collapse at one moment, she now leaned on the wall again and broke into bubbles of laughter. I had heard about hysterics, though I didn't know what they were except that they were something to do with laughing at nothing, and I was wondering whether she was going to " have " them.

From a throat of ashes I asked, " What are you laughing at ? "

" If you c-could s-see yourself. You look so f-funny. Your blouse. And your foot."

I was so relieved at her recovery that I was able to laugh too. " Well, if you had a looking-glass you'd see something else to laugh at. The dye's come out of your hat—it's all over your forehead—black streaks. And your hair's all rats'-tails."

That little spurt of laughter seemed at once to remove a weight and to supply new strength. She came away from the wall, and put one foot slowly in front of the other, and we hobbled a little way. Then she stopped again and looked solemn, or as solemn as she could with a dish-cloth frock, rats'-tails and a streaky face. " D'you know——"

" What ? "

" I believe this is a judgment."

" Judgment ? What is ? "

" This. Yes. A judgment on us. This rain. And losing my money. And losing the way. A judgment on us for stealing. You know what it says in the text —Thou God Seest Me. Well . . ."

I tried to dodge it. " But it wasn't really stealing.

There were miles and miles of that lavender. And three or four stalks wouldn't—— Besides, those we took were growing on the footpath. Not in the field. And after all, we didn't have them."

"Doesn't matter. Makes no difference to what we did. They didn't belong to us. Taking what isn't yours is stealing anyway, whether you keep it or not. We ought not to have done it. Only I was so excited seeing it all like that—all of a sudden. But there you are, you see. Be sure your sins will find you out. And I believe that's what it's for. All this. A lesson to us. I shall remember this for the rest of my life."

I was a little scared, and I covered my scare with annoyance.

"Don't be silly, Freda. Anyway, it's no good thinking about it. That won't alter it. Come on—let's keep going."

We plodded on, and as we went the sun came out and made us look funnier than we had looked in the rain. Somehow or other we struggled up that hill, one dragging pace after another, and then before us, at a little distance, we could see the beginning of the Green. Then came the worst bit. In sight of home, yet so far to go—the whole stretch of the Green, which seemed twice its usual size, between us and it. We walked with sagging knees and the feet of tramps. Freda was lurching more than ever, and when we reached the Green she lurched to one of the public benches and collapsed on it.

"Must sit down."

I hesitated. "I've heard it said you ought never to sit down when you're wet through. You get pneumonia."

"Don't care. Must. Just for a minute or two."

So we sat, wrapped in our individual exhaustion and thirst and distress. After a couple of minutes I said, "We'd better not sit any longer. I'm sure you'll get an awful cold. Come on." I got hold of her, and pulled her, and got her up, and we went plodding on, two bedraggled and apparently drunken objects, rough-dried after being fished out of a pond. At last we reached the centre of the Green, and there, O blessed sight, was the oasis of the public drinking-fountain, and I knew the feeling of the heroes of my adventure-books, lost in the desert, when they saw the dim outline of palms.

I staggered to it in a sleepy run, and fell against it. I had been thinking of it for the last hour, and had arranged what I would do when I reached it—how I would take cups and cups and cups of its cold benedic-tion—glug-glug, glug-glug—one after the other for five minutes. I filled one cup in gasping haste and took it off in two gulps. I filled a second, and drank that more slowly. Then, having filled a third, I was astonished to find that though I had drunk scarcely half a pint, I couldn't drink a third cup. I didn't want any more. I was so astonished that I stood still with the cup in my hand, staring at it. I could not have believed that so raging a desire could so easily be allayed. It was something to remember, and in later life I remembered it and found it useful.

Then on again, and after long minutes the Green came to an end and we crawled into the High Street. And the first thing we saw was Freda's father, who saw us and stared at us with a puzzled frown. Freda gave a long " O-oh," and lurched to him, and grabbed his arm, and collapsed against him. There was the usual temper in his eyes, and he gave us another long and thunderous inspection, and then barked, " And where have you two been all day ? And what on earth have you been up to, to get into this state ? "

Freda told the story in telegram language. " St-stealing lavender, Daddy. Miles and miles away. And he saw us and chased us. A great big stick. And we had to run. And I lost my money. We had to walk all the way home in the rain. Miles and miles."

He looked again at her and at me, and then at the

High Street.   " I can't make out what you're supposed
to be talking about.   But what the devil did you walk
in the rain for ? "

" But, Daddy, we couldn't have got a bus.   We had
no money."

" Wasn't there a station anywhere near ? "

" We saw one somewhere.   But we had no money."

" But where there's a station, there's cabs.   Why
didn't you get one ? "

" But Daddy, I *told* you.   We had no *money*."

" Well, you little fool, you didn't need any.   You
need only have told him to drive home, and Molly
could have paid when you got there."

Her face went blank, and she gave a howl.   " Oh,
Daddy—I never *thought* of that."

" More fool you."   He stopped a four-wheeler that
was ambling by.   " Here—come on—get in.   Both of
you."   He bundled us in and got in with us, and we
drove off to Geneva Street and Lamorna Road.
" Another time, don't be such a resourceless little
idiot."

" I won't, Daddy.   And I'll never pick flowers again,
not even if they are growing on the footpath."

" Flowers ?   I thought you said something about
lavender."

" Yes, it was lavender.   Just like the sea."

" The sea ?   What's that got to do with it ?   You
said footpath."

" Yes.   That's where it was.   Just by the hedge
where the man jumped.   A big black beard.   That's
how I lost my money.   It looked just like the sea—
blue."

" Blue money ?   Black beard ?   What the—— Oh,
shut up, you little fool ! "

She caught my eye, and at his spurt of temper and
the sudden easing of our woes we went off into giggles
which even his glares couldn't stop.

Strange how one common little episode out of a
score can be so suffused by Time with the flush of

magic that it can at any moment, like an old musical-
box or a quavering poem in an Annual of 1830, give
the heart the stab of life. Every summer since then
I have only had to hear the cry of the lavender-woman
—" Will you buy-uy, my sweet blooming lavender ? "
—to be halted by a shock of guilt and a pang of
melancholy.

CHAPTER VI

FLYING ANGEL

AMONG the various figures that made casual and
intermittent appearance in my young life was
an Uncle Paul who wasn't properly an uncle. He was
a nondescript relation whom I liked and sometimes,
in the impudence of youth, felt sorry for without
knowing why I felt sorry. He played the drums in
the orchestra of the Imperial Palace, and the solemn
monotonous throb of those instruments was exactly
suited to his character. He had the vivacity and
perception of a Dutch doll, and with his flat black hair
and blank face and eyes as lively as oysters, he looked
like one. In his general bearing he made curates seem
frivolous. Like most of the adults I knew, he saw life
as a series of Facts, though he seldom perceived them
when they faced him. Peter Bell did at least *see* the
primrose ; Uncle Paul saw only the tip of his nose.
He had just the five senses and overworked none of
them.

He had queer notions about children, and seemed
to have forgotten that he was ever himself a child ;
or perhaps, like many men, he had never known that
state but had been born middle-aged. He thought
boys liked having their hair ruffled backwards, and
liked being heartily banged on the back, and liked
being called whipper-snappers or gay young sparks.

He had a weakness for tittering little jokes, and always expected me to double up with laughter, and when I didn't, he would tell me that a sense of humour was a great thing. The jokes at that time irritated me, but later I perceived that only a man who was essentially good could have found delight in such things.

He was always particular about his appearance, and looked at any time of day as pink and clean as if he had just come from a Turkish bath. He was concerned too about being well dressed, but while his clothes were usually good, his efforts at dressiness were dogged by the imp of Frustration. Those were the days of single stiff collars (or chokers) and by one of those vile tricks which the imp loves to play upon innocent men, Uncle Paul would constantly appear in Correct Town Wear but with his tie riding upon the back edge of his collar —a trifle that had the power of reducing the most august dignity to the level of low comedy.

But he was all good nature and honest impulse, and I recall an afternoon when his good nature opened for me some months of stimulating adventure. He turned up that afternoon in his casual way, without any apparent purpose, and created the usual atmosphere of yawn that was created wherever he was. Then, just as he was going, he asked if I would care to come and see the show at the Palace. There was some discussion as to whether it was quite right for a boy of my age to be taken to a music-hall, but he brushed the discussion aside. He made noises like *Woof* and *Boop*, and said there was no harm in it ; course not ; what an idea. "He can sit in the orchestra with me."

So that evening I had my first music-hall, and experienced a new revelation of real life ; real life expressed through the human body. Uncle Paul called back for me at half-past seven, and I marched along with him to the Palace, feeling sorry, as I went, for the hundreds of dull-faced people who were not going to the Palace. I even felt sorry for those who were going in by the main entrance, because they were going to pay, while *I* was going in free and, further, I was going in by the stage-door in quite a professional way. I hoped I would be seen.

Uncle Paul led me down a side-street, and round to the back, and at a narrow entrance, guarded by a remorseful-looking man in a peaked cap, we went in. We went along a bare stone passage, and then down some stone steps into another passage, where Uncle Paul left his hat and coat. Then into yet another passage, so low that he had to stoop. We went along that little gangway, with a lot of noise going on above us, until we came to about its middle, where there was a little opening. Uncle Paul pushed me into that opening, which was so low that even I had to stoop, and then with a little shock I found myself standing in a blaze of light and a clamour and a little forest of music-stands, and in front of me was a great sea— three waves of it, one above the other—of white faces, from which came a great gush of oranges and cigars. I was in the Imperial Palace orchestra-pit.

With a hand on my shoulder Uncle Paul pushed me along to the corner at the extreme left, and I blundered among the music-stands and the musicians, hot and dazed and happy. Uncle Paul motioned me to a low chair, and told me to keep quiet and not move about, and then began tapping and adjusting his instruments, and adding his solemn noise to the general tumult of tuning. It was so new, so different from the little theatre to which I had been taken for pantomime, and from the Egyptian Hall and St. James Hall, and there were so many points to engage my eyes and observation, that I couldn't pay attention to any one because of a dozen others.

Then, while I was gazing around, the tuning stopped with a snap, and the conductor came in. He was much younger than Uncle Paul ; younger than any of the members of the orchestra, which I thought hardly fair. But he was a lordly and gleaming figure with his glossy white shirt and glossy white collar and white gloves and white camelia in his buttonhole, and I was pointedly admiring him when, as he settled himself in his chair and took up the baton, he looked over in our direction, and nodded and smiled. At first I thought he was smiling at Uncle Paul, but I saw that Uncle Paul had his head down, fiddling with his music. Then I realised that the smile was actually for me. The Conductor of the Imperial Palace orchestra was smiling at me ! It was such an overwhelming honour, and so unexpected, that I blushed all over my face and round the back of my neck.

Then right at my ear came a crash from Uncle Paul's drums, which made me jump in my chair, and the orchestra dashed into the overture. When that was done there was a moment's pause ; then away they dashed into the Introduction for the first turn, and the lights went down, and the great curtain went up, and on came a most dashing lady in short skirts and enormous hat, and with a bosom as big as the class-room map of the hemispheres, who burst into song about waiting in vain in the lane in the rain. Uncle Paul had given me a programme, but it was a list of names that told me nothing. They were all, he muttered, Big Turns, and the house by its applause seemed to confirm this. There were comedians who amused the house by hitting each other, and there were comedians who amused the house by conversing and misunderstanding each other. There were men in evening dress who sang serious songs about dead children, and men in madhouse dress who sang comic songs about dead cats. With all of them the house joined in the choruses, and some of them it seemed anxious to keep for the whole evening. They were brought back to sing again and again.

It was all very different from the pantomime, and from the magic of the Egyptian Hall and the bizarre comedy and equally bizarre pathos of the Moore and Burgess Minstrels, and I wasn't sure that I understood what it was all about. But I felt on the whole that I was having an exciting evening. Until, that is, just after the middle of the evening, and then it became something more than exciting.

At the end of the interval the attendant in gold lace and knee-breeches put a card bearing the number 8 in a slot at the side of the stage, and I saw from my programme that Number 8 was The Great Silvario. The programme didn't say what he was going to do, but the orchestra introduced him in a way that was rather promising. It dashed into a march which I had heard at times on the organ and which I saw from Uncle Paul's music was called *El Capitan*. Then, in the middle of the march, the curtain went up, and I gasped. It went up on a full stage with surrounding curtains of dark blue. On the stage were three trapezes and a horizontal bar of dazzling white. The lighting of the set was a chilly water-blue.

The orchestra broke off its *El Capitan*. Then it blared a long tremulous chord, and on came a slender figure clothed from neck to feet in a close-fitting costume of silver scales. The Great Silvario. He walked as I imagined angels would walk ; that is, he didn't walk ; he moved across the stage, but one scarcely saw his feet touch the ground, nor any undulation of the body. It was as if he swam. He bowed. And the very bow had music in it. With a fling of his arm he indicated the horizontal bar, and the gesture was an invocation as brave and beautiful as the challenge of a sword. He swam to the horizontal bar. He rubbed his feet on a little board. He rubbed his hands on a white silk handkerchief and tossed it aside with an air of farewell to all commonplace everyday things.

The orchestra went into action again, this time with something of an odd and tickling rhythm. From Uncle Paul's music I saw that it was called *Invitation to the Waltz*. Then, though I never saw him move, I saw that he had swung himself to the horizontal bar, and was standing poised on it. In the next second there was a flash of silver, and he was on one of the trapezes, hanging by the legs ; another flash, and he was on the next, and without a pause beyond touching it with his hands, he was on the third, swinging out over the orchestra just above our heads. Then, with its return swing, he shot himself through the ropes of the intervening trapezes, and was standing on the horizontal bar as cool and motionless as though he had never left it.

That, with much variation and amplification, was his act. In it he defied all laws and did the apparently impossible. He made mid-air somersaults. He turned his body three times over, lengthwise, while in flight. He seemed able to impel his body through the air in any direction, and even, while moving, to change direction. His legs were hands with which he caught any swinging bar. His body was a thing which he used for the making of aerial designs and new forms of motion. He went through the air as fluently as song. Most of the time he was living in space between one trapeze and another, with scarcely a moment's rest, making flashes of silver that mingled with the cold blue light and with the insouciant phrases of the *Invitation to the Waltz* until I found myself holding my breath in sheer wonder and joy.

Watching him I knew what poetry was, and what artists meant when they wrote about art. Here, once again, was life-as-it-is, and before that flowing and floating grace my eyes were stung with tears. It was not only itself lovely ; like all lovely things it made everything about it lovely. It threw a shower of happiness over all life. It made the heavy commonplace bodies of the audience lovely. It made the thought of my daily day lovely. It made the members of the orchestra, playing the *Invitation to the Waltz*, lovely. It made even Uncle Paul a lovely companion. As for the shining creature who was creating it all, I was filled with adoration of him.

The turn was only an eight-minute turn, but for me it covered the whole evening. It ended with the usual piece of bravura. Two tall household step-ladders were brought on, and a pair was set at either side of the stage. The top step of each was a little platform about a foot square. The ladder on the left stood a little lower than that on the right. Silvario mounted the taller of the two, though I didn't see him mount —he floated up. He stood on its little platform. The orchestra stopped. He turned his back to the other ladder, bent his body, and stretched his arms behind him. Then he shot them forward ; there was a flash of silver in the air, a crescendo roll from Uncle Paul on the side-drums, and he landed square on the tiny platform of the other ladder. For a second or two he held the triumphant pose, while the orchestra blared a chord ; then swung down to the stage like a snowflake, and bowed himself off.

He took two curtain-calls, and then the orchestra dashed into the " symphony " of the song of the next turn, and the curtain went up on a comic Irishman. But I didn't want to see any more, and though I sat and watched the stage I didn't see anything. My eyes were filled by the vision of Silvario. I wished the whole evening could have been Silvario. I could have watched him for hours. All that followed seemed inane, without light or colour. I was so affected that it must have shown in my face. I heard the trombone, who was sitting next to Uncle Paul, mutter, " Looks as though he's swallowed a lamp."

When the show ended I went out with Uncle Paul, and we struggled through the crowd in the High Street, from which little groups of lads detached themselves and went off playing on mouth-organ or concertina the songs we had heard. As we went along to Geneva Street I had little to say ; I was bemused by what I had seen. But when Uncle Paul asked if I had liked it, I said it had been jolly good ; and when he asked what I had liked best I said, " The Great Silvario, of

course." He said, " Oh. Thought you'd have preferred the comics." I said, " No ; they were just
silly. The Great Silvario was wonderful."

He grunted. " Mm . . . yes. He's not a bad turn.
Quite a good acrobat if you like that kind of thing."

Acrobat ! I hadn't seen any acrobat. I had seen
the marvel of the human body in full living. I had
seen a marvel made of lights and music and form and
motion—and he called the divine creature who made
it, an Acrobat. He went maundering on. " He's not
a bad chap. Pity, though, he can't do something more
sensible. I feel that about all these music-hall people.
Silly way of earning a living."

Creating wonder and beauty every night ; and he
called it Earning a Living and Silly. I felt inclined
to say, " Not half so silly as banging a drum." He
went on, " Yes ; I asked him some time ago what made
him choose that silly——"

I stopped him. " What ! D'you *know* him ? "

" Know him ? Course I do. He lives here. Always
mooning about the Green in the morning."

" He *lives* here ? " I found it hard to realise im-
mediately that he lived anywhere outside that blue
light, and it was astonishing to learn that he lived in
our suburb.

" Yes. Always has done."

" And you *know* him ? "

" To be sure."

I looked at him with, for the first time, respect. He
knew that divine creature. He had stood close to
him. He had talked to him as he was talking to me.
Often and often. And thought nothing of it. I saw
him now as a man of hitherto unperceived qualities
and record. He knew The Great Silvario. He was
at home among sceptres and haloes. I began to see
something of Silvario's own radiance about him, as one
perceives essence of majesty in the man who keeps the
keys of the Crown Jewels or drives the royal coach.
Yes ; if Uncle Paul knew that archangel, and spoke of

his acquaintance so casually, there was no guessing what he didn't know or what he hadn't done in his time. Though none of it could eclipse knowing The Great Silvario. That was enough for any one life. I wondered what it would feel like to be able to say that one knew The Great Silvario. To be with some other boy, looking at one of Silvario's posters, and to be able to say, " Oh, yes—I know him. I often go to his house." But I wouldn't be able to say it as casually as Uncle Paul.

I asked him, " Do you often see him in the day-time ? "

" Pretty often."

" Do you think I could see him some time with you ? "

" You ? What d'you want to see him for ? "

" I want to thank him."

" What for ? "

" For—well—for what I saw him do to-night."

" Mm . . . Rather odd. There's nothing much in his act. And he's a very ordinary chap. Still, if you want to, you can. Come on the Green Saturday morning. Near the Big Pond. About eleven. I'll be having a walk round there. And I expect he'll be somewhere about. He always is."

Saturday morning seemed a long way away, but at last it came. I took very little time in spending my two halfpennies, and at half-past ten I was by the Big Pond, looking all round me at once for any figure that might possibly be The Great Silvario. But the few people round about were all very shapeless and leaden in appearance, and awkward in their movement. No archangel was on the Green just then.

At something past eleven Uncle Paul strolled into the scene, dressed as though for Hyde Park Church Parade, and with his tie behaving with its usual indecency. He greeted me with a nod, and I said, " I haven't seen The Great Silvario anywhere. Do you think he'll come ? "

He said, " Bound to. As regular as clockwork.
There he is now."

I swung round and saw a large figure approaching ;
a large figure in frock-coat, grey trousers, gleaming silk
hat with a curly brim, and silver-headed cane. The
pale face and yellow curly hair were familiar, but what
was chiefly familiar was his walk. Disguised as he was
in those common clothes, he was walking like nobody
else. His body was coming nearer to us, but you could
scarcely see *how* it came. I stood and stared with a
jump of excitement in my chest. Here he was, on our
Green, and I was going to meet him.

Then he was with us, and Uncle Paul was speaking
to him with a jerk of the head at me. " Young
connexion of mine. Brought him to see the show the
other night. Quite taken with your act. Wanted
to meet you." He pushed me forward. " Here
you are—this is The Great Silvario—Mr. Joe
Grummant."

I bowed. I was not dismayed at learning that the
archangel's name was Joe Grummant. I was not
dismayed at seeing the lithe electric flash enclosed in
frock-coat and silk hat. I was not dismayed at finding
that airy figure that sailed and swam and whirled
through the air disguised in the massive, stolid figure
that stood before me. The Great Silvario was for me
so great that he could be as massive as he liked, and
wear any clothes he liked, and carry any harsh or
stupid name, and still he would be as marvellous as
in his silver scales. I bowed and blushed. He looked
down and smiled. Then he looked round the Green.
Then he looked again at me, and said it was a nice
bright morning, and I felt the morning was much
brighter since he had noticed it. I fancy I had an
idea that he would be too great to notice the weather.
He said the Green was a nice place, and there were
some nice walks on it. I said Yes. On the Big Pond
boys were sailing model yachts, and he asked if I had
a yacht and sailed it on the ponds, and I said No. He

was surprised, and said to Uncle Paul, " We must get him one. Boy who lives near ponds *ought* to have a yacht. It's a lot of fun." I thought that was wonderful of him, but I hoped he wouldn't give me a model yacht, because sailing boats on the ponds wouldn't have interested me. He asked if I played chess, and I said I could just play, and he said that was grand. He liked a game of chess himself. It was nice to sit down quiet sometimes and play a quiet game. He didn't like a lot of noise.

I listened to every word of those remarks, and noted them. I was surprised and moved to find that though he was The Great Silvario, he wasn't at all lofty or stand-offish. He was as easy to talk to as Uncle Paul ; easier, indeed ; he didn't insist on the fact that he was older and wiser. He took, as I thought, the trouble to talk simply to me and to suggest that he was just as unimportant as I was. He asked if I ever did anything on the horizontal or parallel bars, and I said I didn't. He said he was working up a new act on the parallel bars, and I would have to come and see it and tell him what I thought of it. He said it didn't look as if it would keep fine all day, and I said No ; it didn't. Conversation then dried up, and we all three stood and ruminated.

Then Uncle Paul said he would be strolling along, and I moved with him, but he waved me off and said, " You can stop and talk to Mr. Grummant." I felt a little awkward. I didn't think Mr. Grummant would want to be bothered with me, and I shifted from one foot to the other. But Mr. Grummant was very kind. He said, " That's right, son. You stop and talk to me. Let's take a walk."

Another jump in the chest. Taking a walk on the Green with The Great Silvario in full view of everybody. . . . For a moment I was overcome and stood struck. Then I saw that his great bulk had already floated a few paces away, and I ran to catch him up. We went in silence for some time. Then he said, " Well, son,

G

so you liked my show. Would *you* like to do that kind
of thing ? "

I said I thought it must be wonderful to be able to
do those things, but I knew they would never be
possible to me, and I wasn't sure I would want to do
them, perhaps because I never could ; but I'd like to
be able to do something *like* them. He said, " What
sort of thing ? " and I said I didn't know except that
when I grew up I'd like to do something that wasn't
ordinary Work. Not the wonderful things he could do,
perhaps, but something—something—something. . . .
He said, " Ah, to be sure."

We stood against the railings of the Big Pond, and
he said the ponds made the Green much nicer than
other Greens or Parks, and I said Yes, they did. He
said it was nice to see a lot of water, and I said it was.
A silence of a minute or more followed that ; then, to
make conversation, I said, " What a lovely place the
Imperial Palace is inside."

" Think so ? Not bad. But not a patch on the
Empire or Alhambra. Wait till you see them.
Gorgeous places."

I asked him where they were, and he said they were
in Leicester Square, and I asked where that was, and
he said it was Up West. I asked, " Have you performed there ? " and he said he had worked both
houses several times, but neither of them was a Good
Audience. It was only ballet that really went in those
places. Nor was the Royal Aquarium a Good Audience. But the Canterbury and the South London and
the Oxford—they were Audiences, they were. And
what houses !

I didn't understand all that, and he must have seen
my puzzled frown because, in his greatness, he condescended to explain to me in simple terms that a
House meant every seat occupied, and an Audience
was Good when it was lively and attentive, and when
it followed your act and was up to all your good work
and down on you if you made a mistake. He'd rather

have boos and cat-calls than play to a lot of fish.   It
was easier to play to an audience that didn't like you
than to an audience that didn't pay any attention at
all.   Audiences were Good or Bad, Hot or Cold, and
it was funny how they varied from night to night, and
how, though they were made up of hundreds of people
of different sorts who didn't know each other, they were
always either one or the other.   Monday night always
meant a Cold Audience and Saturday night always a
Hot one.   You'd be surprised.

I wasn't surprised.   I was only profoundly interested
in anything The Great Silvario condescended to say to
me.   He broke off just then.   Near us some boys were
throwing stones into the trees at the birds, and he
broke off to shout at them.   It was a shout as large as
himself, and what with the shout and his size, the boys,
after one look, dropped their stones and slunk off.
" I don't like to see that," he said.   " I don't think
it's right.   There's room for all of us on this earth, and
the animals have as much right to live as we have.
Don't you think so ? "   I said I did, and I thought it
wonderful that the archangel should concern himself
with little things of that sort.   It struck an echo in
my mind of something from the Bible Class lessons
about not one sparrow shall fall to the ground without . . .

We walked on in another silence.   Then he asked,
" How old are you, son ? . . . Eleven, eh ? Nice
age to be.   Wish I was eleven again."

I knew from my books that the great had their
eccentricities, but I couldn't understand why anybody
leading his real life should have so eccentric a wish as
that.   I asked, " Don't you like your present life, Mr.
Gr— Mr. Silvario ? Don't you like what you're
doing ? "

He said, " I love it.   It's all I want to do."

I said, " I should think anybody would be happy
who could do those things.   To be grown up and able
to live like that and——"

" Yes. I *am* happy. When I'm doing 'em."

" How did you come to do it, Mr. Silvario ? How did you learn ? "

" I never did learn. It just come natural to me. I drifted into it and it grew in me. As a boy I was always doing monkey-tricks. Climbing trees and jumping from one to the other. Then when I was about twelve I got in with a circus-troupe. I played truant from school one day to see 'em. And never went back. I went off with 'em. I was with 'em about four years, doing hand-springs and cart-wheels in the ring, and tight-rope stuff and balancing stuff. Then I went on the halls with a couple of other lads. Then I struck out an act of me own. What I'm doing now."

" I think it's wonderful. I've never seen anything like it in all my life. Aren't you ever afraid of an accident ? "

He laughed. " Isn't time for thinking of that. And nobody who did think of it would be any good for that work. You don't think in that work, anyway. You don't think of anything. If you did, you'd make a slip. You let your mind go, and leave it to the body to do it all by itself. Then you're all right. Do you like lemonade ? " I said I did. " Come in, then, and have a lemonade. Or a lime-juice. That's my house." He pointed to one of the small Georgian cottages bordering the Green, and we went across to it. I felt more jumps in the chest. I was going into the archangel's home. I was going to drink his lemonade ; to see the rooms he spent his time in, and sit in the chairs he sat in. It was a miraculous Saturday Morning.

The furniture of the house, as I see it now, was commonplace ; the kind of stuff one saw in the windows of the furniture-shops in the High Street ; but I thought it splendid then ; a right royal setting for a right royal creature. We went into a sitting-room, and he called down a passage to an Agnes to bring two glasses of lemonade. In a few moments Agnes,

an elderly woman, brought them on a tray. She was
an odd-looking woman, outside my experience, and I
couldn't at first "make her out." She looked like a
suburban housewife in an unusually flighty mood, as
though she might at any moment break into a dance.
Her face was old but her hair was bright yellow, and
her clothes looked as though she was just off to a party
or had just come back from one. He indicated me and
said, " Young friend of mine. He thinks I'm wonderful." Agnes made a " face " and said, " So you are,
you big sausage." When she had gone, he said, " My
housekeeper. She used to be a Big Turn when she
was young. Light comedy songs."

I drank some of the archangelic lemonade, and he
threw open a french window and said, " The garden,"
and stepped out. I followed him. He said, " I like
a bit of garden. Even a small one. I think a garden's
nice." I said I thought so too. I was prepared to
think anything he thought. It was really rather a
large garden, with a central lawn and flower-borders
and a tree or two. At the bottom, behind a line of
bushes, I saw a long shed with a glass roof, which I
thought was a green-house. He saw me looking at it
and said, " My gymnasium." I looked at it again,
with awe. " Might I just look in ? "

" Course you may if you want to."

We went down to it, and he unlocked it, and I
looked in. It had parallel bars, horizontal bars,
trapezes, vaulting-horse, bar-bells, fencing-foils and
other fixtures. He moved about it, touching things, a
pat here and a soft stroke there. Then we came out,
and went back to the sitting-room and our lemonade.
He moved about the room, here and there, and I was
afraid I was a nuisance and in the way ; but from later
visits I found he spent the whole day like that, mooning and pottering. At last he sat down and told me
to sit down. He pointed to a small table in the
corner and said, " My chess-table." I gave it a mental
bow. He pointed to a photograph on the mantel-

shelf and said, " My mother." I had hardly expected
him to have had a mother. I saw no books about the
place, and I learned later that he had never " read a
book," and only occasionally flipped over the newspaper. There was a piano, and I asked if he played.
He said he just strummed now and then when he had
nothing to do ; just any tunes that came into his head.

Other little details were thrown up during the next
half-hour about his life and habits, and I stored each
detail away with the care of a collector. I learned
that he had often appeared on the Continent, and
spoke four languages—" in a rough and ready way "
—which I thought an additional matter of marvel.
He had never smoked or drank, and I resolved that I
never would ; a resolution to which I held till I was
fourteen. He never took a real substantial dinner.
In the course of the day he had five light meals. On
getting up he drank a pint of water, and had half an
hour in the gym. His breakfast was tea without milk,
fish, eggs and raw fruit. At about half-past ten he
had beef-tea and dry toast. At two o'clock a cutlet,
a green vegetable, and more raw fruit. At seven
o'clock weak tea, an egg-dish, and toast ; and after
the show a supper of chicken and a bowl of salad, and
at bed-time a glass of hot milk.

After another long silence he said, " So you don't
want to do ordinary Work. What do you call ordinary
Work ? "

" I said " Well . . . business. I don't want to go
to an office every day or a shop."

" I see. But business is where the money is made."

" Yes, but that isn't everything."

" Perhaps not. But you've got to have it. And
business is where you get it. Look at Mr Wildon, the
draper. Look at his enormous place. Employs two
hundred people. And three years ago he had one little
shop in a side-street. That shows what business is."

" I don't see much in that," I said. " It's not really
interesting. It's only selling things."

" Makes the money, though. Don't you want to make money ? "

" I've never thought about it."

" You ought to. Besides, it's not only the money. It leads to all sorts of things. Mr. Wildon's mayor now. And they say he'll be in Parliament next year. That's doing something interesting, isn't it ? "

" No. Not what I mean. Not like you're doing. And he doesn't look as though he had much money. Lives in a little house like ours. And goes about all shabby and rides in trams. I should have thought he'd have had a big house and a brougham."

" He puts his money back in the business."

" Then he hasn't really got any. You haven't got money if it's in a money-box or in the bank. You've only got it when you're spending it."

" Well, there's something in that. I see you've got ideas. You ought to do something."

" But I don't want to do anything dull, like business. I want to do something special. Not the wonderful things you do, but something like I felt when watching you."

" Ah, yes. I know."

I experienced repeated gusts of astonishment at finding myself sitting there in The Great Silvario's house, and talking away to that divine creature as though I had always known him, as though he were just anybody, and getting on with him as easily as I got on with Freda. It was incredible. But it was a fact. During the intervening days after seeing his act he had been a remote divinity, unapproachable save with a hundred reverences. And now there I was, getting on with him like anything, and he liked me, or was very cleverly pretending to. I found later that he really did like me so far as he was capable of like or dislike. He accepted me as something that was, and the fact that I was a boy of eleven wasn't the kind of fact that had for him any implication or significance.

At one o'clock I got up and said they'd be expecting

me at home. He said, " That's right, son. Punctu-
ality. Mustn't keep your dinner waiting. Come and
see me another day. Any time you like. I'm always
here up to half-past seven. Or come and see the show
again next time I'm working the Palace. If your
uncle can't bring you, come to the stage-door and ask
for me, and see the show from the wings."

I gasped my thanks, and said that would be Wonderful if I really might, and he said to be sure I might.
Any time. And he came to the door with me, the
massive blond archangel, and opened the door for me,
and dropped a shilling in my hand (a shilling—more
money than I had ever possessed) and said, " Ta-ta,
son," and went indoors.

That meeting began a regular Saturday Morning
acquaintance, with a routine of meeting on the Green,
going back with him, having lemonade, and talking
about Life and agreeing that it was nice to be out in
the early morning or that it was not nice to have to
meet rude people. Sometimes I shared his seven
o'clock meal, and those meals were events that remain
in my memory like coloured lantern slides. However
great his housekeeper may have been as a music-hall
artiste, she was equally great as a caterer of schoolboy
teas. Whenever she knew I was coming, she provided
the perfect and ever-memorable summer or winter Tea.

The table was always fully laid when I arrived ; a
good touch, since it gave the eye a mass effect of colour
and an anticipatory thrill of the individual satisfactions
to follow ; and it certainly was a table. I was the
only guest, but looking at the table one would have
said that she expected half a dozen schoolboys. Most
of the spread was of things that Silvario never touched.
It was all for me. What happened to the surplus I
never knew. In summer there were jellies red and
gold ; strawberries and cream or raspberries ; a bowl
of cherries ; a bowl of stewed greengages ; jam-puffs ;
the pink-and-white of iced cake ; honey, marmalade,
and jams crimson and yellow and black. In winter

there were the honey and the jams and the iced cake, with the golden-brown of sausage-rolls, the brown and cream of crumpets, all sorts of potted meats, and toast and Swiss Roll and brandy-snaps and what not. Her instincts as a caterer must have been cruelly thwarted under Silvario's sparse feeding, and perhaps that explained her lavish display on my visits. She may have made them an excuse for furnishing a table that she herself could look at with approval.

Those occasions when I was allowed to go with him and sit in his dressing-room, and see him from the wings, were something to think about, each of them, long afterwards. His performance never ceased to be wonderful. From the wings I saw things you couldn't see from the house. I saw the real work behind the act ; I saw the effort it required. Where, from the house, you saw airy grace, I saw from the wings the sweat, and the cataleptic eye, and I heard his grunts, and the creak of the resin, and his voice counting to the music, and the crack of the trapeze-bars as he landed on them—things that were drowned for the house by the *Invitation to the Waltz*. I saw how every step across the stage was calculated ; how everything was in position to the half-inch ; how the apparent floating from the ground to the high horizontal bar was a spring that used every muscle. But it was still a wonderful act, and it moved me the tenth time from the wings as it had done the first time from the house.

I continued to be surprised that so great and divine a creature should be willing to let me go and see him, and to listen to my talk, and to be so simple in his talk to me, and I once mentioned this to one of my elders, who had met him with me when I was proudly marching with him on the Green. I said how kind it was of him to make me so easy with him, and to talk to me not as though I were a schoolboy, as most adults did, but as though we were equal and he were the same age as myself. And I got the reply, " He is." Which didn't seem to me to make sense. Not at that time.

And I continued to be puzzled by the difference between The Great Silvario and Joe Grummant. Until at last I realised that they really were two different people. Joe Grummant wasn't alive. He never was alive at any time. He was only a body, and it wasn't until Silvario took possession of the body that it became all that it was on that blue-lit stage. When Joe Grummant took off his day clothes, he took off not only the clothes but Joe Grummant as well. When he undressed and put on the shining livery and the name of Silvario, something occult happened. There was a transformation. Joe Grummant vanished, and the crystal, mercurial Silvario was born.

There actually was that transformation. I saw it happen before my eyes each time I sat in his dressing-room. At one minute I saw the bored, sleepy Joe Grummant with his clothes half off, and the next minute, with the livery of Silvario half on, the face was filled from within by light. The eyes shone. The big hands became fluttering leaves. With the disappearance of Joe Grummant went too the massive figure, and in its place was a slim, swift figure as supple as a sapling. He was at once smaller and taller—taller by some spiritual luminosity that gave him an outline. Under the change the skin glistened, the muscles were as fluent as little waves. The very hair became lustrous, and when his dresser had adjusted the last strap and button, the shining creature that stood in the middle of the room had no more relation to Joe Grummant than to a tram-car.

I did not then know anything of the occult property of the mask in the revelation of character, but I was seeing it in operation. That silver costume was his mask, and the mask with him was not a concealment ; it was, as with so many people, a window through which he could express his real self. When he was wearing frock-coat, trousers and silk hat, he was naked and ashamed and inarticulate. When he was stripped, with no covering save a skin-tight dress of silver silk, he was clothed and in his right mind, and could release himself, and his body could find the speech that his tongue could not. But all I then knew was that he was two different people, and that I had seen the exact minute of the fairy-tale change from drab nobody to illustrious prince. That silver silk was the only dress he should ever have worn.

I knew him for a little over a year. Then that apparently robust and impervious frame went into a decline, as athletes in the perfection of fitness sometimes do; and in a month or so he was dead. And that form which I had known as fluent silver lay in his sitting-room frozen in the white darkness of marble. He who lived only in lovely movement was still. He lay bound like Samson. Stillness, which in life had been death to him, had captured him for ever. His genius had been his lithe body and the fire that played through its muscles and nerves. And the fire was out, and there was nothing but a rigid shape, and the eye's memory of swallow-skims through ice-blue light and flashes through the air of a human sword.

And now, whenever I hear half a dozen bars of the *Invitation to the Waltz*, it brings to me a poetry far keener than the poetry of a young girl attending her first dance.

CHAPTER VII

GOOD-BYE FOR EVER

MUSING in that Bond Street Gallery on what I knew of Kate Greenaway's childhood, I recalled her notes on the children's parties she attended at Islington, where everybody was better dressed than herself and where she felt always shy; and that memory brought a memory of my own first party. It was Freda's birthday-party when she was eleven, and

she asked if I would go. Parties were things I had
only heard about ; excepting Freda, I had no friends
and so never had invitations to things of that sort. I
thought I would like to go to a party, and I went, but
after that first experience I decided that I didn't like
a lot of people gathered together to do the same thing
at the same time ; a decision I have held ever since.

Her birthday was November. The party began at
four o'clock and lasted till about nine, and at the end
they all said it had been a very nice party. I suppose
it was. Since it was Freda's, it would have been ;
she always managed, wherever she was, to spread her
quiet delight in everything to others. For myself, it
had only the interest of novelty.

It was held in two upstair rooms of the Lamorna
Road Bedlam. Their folding-door had been folded,
and the tea was laid in one room and the other was
reserved for the Fun. The party assembled in the
Fun room. There were a few boys, very smart and
starched, who took no notice of me and little notice of
Freda or the other girls ; they gave their notice to
each other and to the tea-table. The rest of the
company was girls. Freda, with her black hair and
her face without a touch of colour, looked seraphic in
a " party " frock of electric-green with white muslin
collar, short puffed sleeves of white muslin, white
stockings, green shoes and amber sash and amber
hair-ribbon. But most of her guests outshone her.

I had never seen in one place such an assembly of
angelic and exquisitely dressed girls. Though I did
not really see them as girls. What I saw was coloured
frocks ; the radiance lent by unusual clothes to black
and golden curls ; the silk and lace and ribbons ;
fabrics of yellow and white and vermilion. They
looked as though they had come from homes as
enchanted and out-of-the-world as themselves ; or
perhaps from conservatories. One or two of them I
had seen before, in the street with Freda, but the
alchemy of dress had wrought such a change that they

seemed to be not themselves but distillations, etherealised matter, or their astral selves. The sight of them later in the evening, standing in a group at the end of the room, set my capricious fancy on another line and linked them not with conservatories, or with anything ethereal, but with certain pictures I had seen at home of quite different things—the coloured plates of marvellously garnished dishes in one of my favourite books —an illustrated Mrs. Beeton.

Before the tea Freda showed some of her presents— a work-basket which could cover half the table or be folded into ten inches ; an ivory penholder with, in the handle, a tiny magnifying-glass which, when you put it to your eye, gave you a clear photographic view of Shanklin Chine ; a fold-up writing-case complete with unleakable ink-bottle ; a silver bracelet ; a pen-wiper in a case of Whitby jet ; a scarlet leather purse with silver clasps and two new half-crowns in it ; a coral necklace ; a bedroom clock in the form of a Swiss chalet ; a box of twelve tablets of scented soap in the shape of kittens ; and a Magic Lantern. All of them, I guessed, except the Magic Lantern, would be in her satchel next day.

The tea-table was a Production, the centre-piece a noble iced cake with eleven lighted candles, sunk in a bed of chrysanthemums. The plate of each guest was enclosed in a circlet of Michaelmas daisies. The general effect of the room was of dark colour and warmth. The silver and china sparkled and shone, and the fire in the twilight danced on the brass fire-irons and the brass fender and the silver photo-frames and the plush curtains, and harmonised with the odours of tea and toast and cake and fruit, and made one of those highly-charged moments when what is at other times the common detail of the daily day become frankincense and myrrh.

The Production, I learned, was the work of the iron-chinned, steel-eyed Molly, who waited on the party with the air of a prison wardress prepared at any moment for mutiny. The girls quickly showed their mundane reality, and kept her well occupied with serving. I had never imagined that such frail and blossom-like creatures could stuff so substantially. They went so far beyond the boys that most of these were sitting sated and glum while the blossoms were still stuffing.

I sat between Freda and a blossom with orange curls in a frock of blue velvet ; a blue so deep that it seemed to be blue in mourning. I found her dull. She spoke only twice, and then to ask me, sweetly enough, to pass something. Looking about the table with judicial eyes I decided that Freda was in looks no match for the blossoms, but from their eyes and their voices I judged that none of them was worthy to be matched in character with her. The voices were aloof and assured ; the eyes were blank. Their attraction could dazzle, but only for five minutes. Freda, like good bread, was satisfying always. Once or twice during the feast I caught her sidelong glance, and she gave me a nod and a little crinkle at the corner of the mouth which I knew were meant to say, " Sorry you find them dull, but they're schoolfellows of mine, and I have to invite them 'cos they invite me to their parties, but you and I can talk when it's over, and don't mind about the silly games, they'll be disappointed if we don't have them. I'll be playing the piano when we've done, and perhaps you'll like that bit. Cheer Up, Funny One."

After tea we moved into the other room for the Fun, which began with Freda being asked to play. She first played two things which she said were by some-body called Chaminade, and then something which she said was the Third Movement of Mozart's Sonata in B Flat—something so gossamer and happy that it was as though fresh air had been set singing. I wished the Fun could have been nothing but Freda playing, but after that we had to have games, none of which I knew. Some of them were table-games and some of them games in which you had to do things—the old games of

Postman's Knock, Honey Pots, Puss-in-the-corner, Nuts in May, Musical Chairs. Then we had songs by those who could sing and those who couldn't, and a boy who had brought a dulcimer gave us a performance on it.

Then Molly and Freda's scowling father fixed a bed-sheet across the folding-door, and the Magic Lantern was rigged up on a small table set on top of a packing-case, and Freda gave her show. The slides were views of the Alps and Rome and Athens, and I didn't accompany them with witty patter or stories : I assisted only by standing beside her at the lantern and handing up the slides.

At half-past eight, Molly, still with the air of handling obstreperous captives, brought in " refreshments," jellies, goblets of boiled custard, lemonade, fruit, cheese-cakes, macaroons, and Freda's brother Carlo, a languid man of seventeen, looked in and for five minutes affably condescended to be seen among the kids and to sample the refreshments. At nine o'clock the party broke up, and they went home, and Freda and I were alone, and I was glad. Parties, I thought, were all right for those that liked them, but they weren't anything like as interesting as just mooning about and talking to her. They seemed to be only a substitute for something else, but I couldn't think what it was. It was so pleasant to be alone with her again, as we always were, that I felt as if she had been away and we were meeting after an absence.

When they were gone, leaving the house simmering with the bright fume of spent pleasure, I went upstairs with her to her " library," to borrow a book. We were always exchanging books, and her collection, though different in its items, was very much like my little lot. Those who didn't know much about girls and their private life sometimes expressed surprise at her books and thought them unusual ; but they were not so unusual. They did not include a single " girl's " book, but the collection was not in that respect unique.

Many a girl's bookshelf might be mistaken for her brother's.

Among the things in her bookcase, which was on the upper landing because there was no space for it in the room she shared with her second sister, were *King Solomon's Mines, Thaddeus of Warsaw, Old St. Paul's, Rookwood, D'Aulnoy's Fairy Tales, Boyhood of Great Men, The Iron Pirate, Round the World in Eighty Days, Tanglewood Tales,* a volume of *Chums, The Lady of the Camelias* (I don't know what that was doing there or whether Daddy knew about it), *Pride and Prejudice, Wuthering Heights, Jane Eyre, Selborne, Bevis, Peter Simple, Huckleberry Finn, Heroes of Asgard, Barry Lyndon, Music and Morals.* None of these was her brother's. All were her own, bought by herself or selected as presents from aunts and uncles. Not the Girl's Bookshelf designed by publishers or school-teachers, but not at all unusual. Looking at it and remembering the kind of thing she carried in her satchel, one would have suspected its owner of being a tomboy rather than what she was.

After I had selected *Old St. Paul's* we sat on the stairs, and she weighed up the party, and decided that she'd had a very satisfactory birthday ; not as good as when she was eight but better than last year's. We then went into one of our discussions of Life and its problems. One of the problems (hers) was whether a glass of water when you were thirsty was better than food when you were hungry—or the other way round. From my experience in the lavender episode I voted certainly that water in thirst was a more thrilling experience than food in hunger. From that we got on to physical sensation, and why a pleasant physical sensation made you find everything, including people, much nicer than at other times. If you were cold on a cold day, things weren't so nice as when you were warm. When you were eating strawberries and cream you could like almost anybody, but if you were hungry or had a pain in the leg, even the people you liked weren't very interesting. The feeling of after-bath, with clean clothes on, made you quite nice to people even when they weren't nice to you. It was funny. It needed thinking about. We thought about it for ten seconds, and gave it up.

She switched to another matter. " Did you like the girl in blue with the curls that sat next to you ? "

" Well . . ." I hesitated, and said the best thing I could about her. " Well, she was very pretty."

" Yes, isn't she ? But she's an awful thief."

" A what ? "

" A thief."

" What—that girl ? A thief ? "

" Yes. She'll steal anything you leave near her— money, sweets, bracelets—anything."

" D'you mean that ? You mean she steals things ? "

" Yes."

" What for ? Is she so poor ? She didn't look poor."

" No. She has more pocket-money than most of us. They're quite well off."

" What makes her do it then—a wicked thing like that ? "

" I don't know. She's had three things out of my satchel when I left it near her. I caught her twice. She'd have had one of my presents this evening if she'd had a chance."

" But . . . she could be sent to prison for that."

" I know."

" Can't her father and mother stop her ? "

" They don't know about it. Only us girls know."

" Haven't you reported her to the head-mistress ? "

" We don't like to."

I was silent for a few moments, digesting the shock of that revelation and Freda's serene acceptance of the fact. It was for me a step in knowledge to learn that beauty could go with wrong-doing. The very look of the word Thief had always brought me an image of somebody mean and furtive and thin, with pinched

H

features and beady eyes and soiled skeleton fingers. And now I learned that a thief could be a sweet creature with orange curls and melting eyes and full lips and white hands. I had heard it said that Beauty was only skin-deep but I had not believed it. I had believed that beautiful people—I had seen very few —were beautiful all through, and that it came from within. All the people I knew were what they seemed to be. The good ones looked good and the wrong ones looked wrong. Freda's revelation presented me with a phenomenon, and I wasn't used to phenomena. It upset me, and remembering the girl's face I felt a little sick.

" But can't you do anything about it ? " I asked. " She might do it in a shop and get caught, and then they'd send for the police and—— Will she grow up like it ? Can't you all tell her that if she does it again you'll report her ? "

" No. We can't very well. She's such a nice girl. We all like her. It doesn't matter anyway. We don't give her any chances now. We keep an eye on her. She knows we know. And she doesn't care. Isn't it funny the way people are ? I think they're *so* interesting."

" Perhaps. But I shouldn't think she'd be a very nice friend."

" Oh, she isn't a friend of mine. I wouldn't be telling even you about her if she were. None of them are really friends of mine. I just know them—that's all. You're my only friend."

" I'm glad I am."

" So'm I. You're better than any of them."

We roamed over other " funny " fields of Life. Sitting on the stairs at the top of the house induced an intimacy not given by our usual meeting-places. It made us ruminative and reflective as men become under the confluence of midnight and the last night-cap. She began to talk of music, and how everybody who wrote music wrote it differently. It was all music ;

yet nobody's was like anybody else's, and if you had six pages of music without knowing who wrote them, you only had to play them over and would know at once that one was Bach's and one was Mozart's and one was Schumann's, and so on. That was funny ; that every man could make the same thing and yet make it differently. I said something about voices when people were talking, and she said Yes ; every voice, if it only said How Are You ? said it in its own music which wasn't like any other. And then I said I didn't know if I was talking silly, but had she ever noticed what I called the music of everyday—that every single thing, when it moved, had its own music ; that it made a noise in its own what's-it—its own— (" Key " she said) and I said, " Yes, that's it. And you can never mistake the sound of one thing for the sound of another. Directly you hear it, even if you can't see it, you know what it is. Like," I went on, " the music of bacon frying, a quite different sound from sausages frying—or beating up an egg—the scrape of a chair-leg—the pouring of water—a cat rushing about on carpet—a dog pattering on oil-cloth—the twenty different notes of twenty different knockers— horse's hoofs on wood-paving—the shooting of a sack of coals—the——"

She took it up with, " Yes—and the crackle of dead cinders—the creak of a particular door in your house —the turn of a key in a door, so that you know just which door—the rustle of paper—the movement of a pen—of a clothes-brush—of a pencil rolling down a table."

And I added, " Yes—and the buttering of toast— moving a teaspoon in a saucer—shutting the lid of a desk—the different kinds of feet on pavement, high heels and thick boots and slippers—the swish of a tree against a window—the different rattle of different windows."

" Yes—and the striking of a match—or dropping a book—or sharpening a knife—or running a sewing-

machine. Yes—all different, and you never mistake
them. Isn't it queer? Everything, when you come
to think about it, is music. It makes life more exciting,
doesn't it?"

I agreed that it did, and then a voice below said it
was time Freda was in bed, which meant that it was
time for me to go. I couldn't give her a birthday-
present; it had been a bad week with jam-jars and
visitors. So I gave her what I could—a halfpenny
birthday-card which she accepted with delight and
said she would pin over her bed.

Then I said Good-night, and went home from my
first party—the first of the three I have attended in
fifty-seven years.

. . . . .

Like most children I led in those days a double life;
a fact life and a daydream life; and sometimes they
synchronised and fused, so that I was in both at the
same time and hardly aware of it. I lived in the
pleasant fact of Geneva Street and the exciting fact of
Freda, and at the same time I lived in other scenes
with quite different people. In my general life I was
at once happy and unhappy. When I had every
reason for being happy, I was discontented. When
conditions were enough to make anybody miserable I
was happy. But if I couldn't always enjoy myself,
I could always, at a distance, enjoy other people.
Everybody's life in scope, action, outlook, surroundings,
seemed so much more interesting than mine, that I was
always picking out people in the High Street or on the
Green, and playing at changing identities with them.
I used them as a resource to supply to either of my
states what was lacking, and made myself one of them
in a serial novelette which I carried on by instalments
for weeks at a time. I felt that if I could leave my
own everyday life and enter their interesting lives and
use their opportunities it would be as exciting as getting
into a book. It would be actually doing what I did

in imagination in going through the doors of the rooms in that coloured picture-book.

The scenes of the novelette were as varied as the characters with whom I changed. Sometimes it was the streets I knew, but of a century or two centuries back ; sometimes it was set in the present, sometimes in the future. And sometimes it moved to some far-off place thrown up by the geography class, and chosen for the plangent syllables of its name—Antananarivo, Trincomalee, Zanzibar, Ecuador, Saskatchewan, Nicaragua, Cambodia, Venezuela, Costa Rica, Khamskhatka, Seringapatam.

I had, as I say, a keen sense of the legend of things and of people, and certain local settings evoked a special kind of story which I felt were apt to those settings. The eighteenth-century corners of our suburb held numbers of little dark passages and yards with one pale bracket-lamp at the corner half-lighting patches of them. Those lamps, dropping their thin light into the crowding shadows, expressed for me all the mystery of town-night, and in those corners I set my imagined characters in the London of Hogarth, whose pictures I had seen in a High Street print-shop, and gave them a part in grotesque episodes and midnight encounters. Sometimes my imagination went more Hogarthian than I meant it to go, and brought an agreeable thrill of real fright.

The dark waste of the Green at night, with a high wind enamelling the sky to the tone of black marble, demanded heroic hair's-breadth stuff, and the long serial I set around it was full of gallant cavaliers and sweeping seventeenth-century sword-and-cloak affairs. The High Street, with its stir of gentle life, and the lamplight falling in broken pieces into the puddles of the road, was a setting for more homely doings. Some of them I set in the shops—in the big drapery store whose overhead cash-railway played an important part in the story ; in the tea-and-coffee blender's ; in the piano shop ; in the red and green window of the chemist ; in the household store, and particularly in the toy-shop.

The upper window of that shop always fascinated me. Its curtains were never drawn, and from the other side of the street I could see corners of a domestic interior—part of a wall with gay pictures and a cuckoo-clock, part of a piano, a fireplace, part of a table covered with table-games, and a woman sitting at it, and two children whom I never saw in the street. The glass between it and the street removed it from every-day life, and made it like a picture with the window as a frame. If any of the people moved, it struck me like magic. I built many an unwritten serial story around that room. Because of its faint hint of other-world, it seemed a fit setting for all manner of fantastic event, and more than one of those dreams provided, twenty years later, the foundation of short stories.

The only person of the fact-world who was ever included in the dramatis personæ of those serials was Freda. I was beginning to realise that Freda and I were very special friends. Not that I knew much of friendship by personal experience, but from my observ-ation of other pairs of friends I did not perceive that they were as important to each other as we were. In her company my rather bare life felt fully furnished, and while, through most of my daily hours, I wanted to push the clock-hands forward, when I was with her I wanted them to stand still. Being with her was at once soothing and stimulating ; she made me all alive ; every minute was charged with some sweet exhalation that made all things better than they were. I didn't understand it, and I·didn't try to. And I certainly didn't understand how she came to belong to that knockabout family, and why they couldn't see how special she was.

There was a day when I realised how very special she was to me. Winter it must have been, because I remember I was going down Geneva Street when I saw her come burning along its length in a scarlet coat and

able suburban present between young friends who were separating; you could get one for sixpence in the Crystal Arcade. But I hadn't got sixpence. So I could only stand and give her my eyes until the red dot was sucked into the horizon and obliterated.

That night I put the Keepsake under my pillow. Freda was going away. Only for a month, she said. But after that she would soon be thirteen, and then she would completely go away. For years, which was the same as For Ever. I lay in bed thinking of Going Away . . . Gone — Going Away . . . Gone. Paris . . . France . . . Abroad . . . Far, Far Away. Not to see her lurching down the street any more. Not to see that flickering face and unruly hair. Not to hear her gurgle. To have nobody to tell things to and get the understanding gleam.

Just before going to sleep I realised that I was thinking selfishly. For her sake I ought to be glad. I ought not to be thinking of what it meant to me; I ought to think of what it meant to her; it was probably going to mean something very good, and I ought to share her excitement and rejoice with her. But I wasn't strong enough to keep my mind in that direction and away from myself. I could only keep recalling all the things we had done together, all the hundred delightful things she had said; and they added up to Going Away and Gone for Ever. That seemed to be Life's arithmetic. I had always known arithmetic was nonsense.

CHAPTER VIII

GROWING PAINS

WAITING in that Bond Street gallery, thinking of Kate Greenaway, who was so aptly born in the spring and so aptly died near Christmas, the

season of her *Almanacks* ; thinking of her, I thought
of her contemporary Randolph Caldecott, and then
of the gracious and sprightly Hugh Thomson, with
whom, in her later years, she had a joint show. And
then I thought of that company of black-and-white
artists who so delightfully embellished the books of
the 'nineties, and the early years of this century.
To-day the illustrated novel, save for an occasional
de luxe edition with woodcuts, is " out," and so to-day
we have no illustrators. But at that time almost
all books carried illustrations—the six-shilling novel
(sold at 4*s.* 6*d.*), the new novels published at 3*s.* 6*d.*
(sold at 2*s.* 8*d.*) and even some of the paper-covered
sixpennies (sold at 4½*d.*) which all publishers then
issued. The demand produced the artists, and I
recalled the work of Edmund J. Sullivan, of Garth
Jones, H. R. Millar, Claude Shepperson, Herbert
Railton, Joseph Pennel, Fred Pegram, Herbert Cole,
Henry Ospovat, Maurice Grieffenhagen, the two
Heath Robinsons, the two Brocks, the Detmolds,
Gordon Browne, Byam Shaw, F. H. Townshend,
Frederick Griggs, Edmund New, Anning Bell.

And those names took me to the year when I was
sixteen and still living in Geneva Street. I was working sullenly in a city office, and I had sold my first
short-story, and the bookshops were displaying books
illustrated by those men which I couldn't buy, and the
street-organs were playing *Hiawatha* (not by Coleridge-
Taylor), and young people were dancing the cake-
walk and the two-step, and the High Street was
humming with the brilliant new electric tram-cars,
and I had made the acquaintance by letter of my first
Author, and he had invited me to spend my summer
holiday with him at Vernon on the Seine, and I
couldn't go because I hadn't anything like the fare,
and he sent me the money.

And then from that Kate Greenaway magic lantern
came a picture of myself in the Author's cottage at
Vernon, and I recalled the getting there by night

boat from Newhaven to Dieppe and thence to Rouen.
At Rouen I had to change stations. I had only my
school French, and though I had taken prizes for it
I hadn't really got it. I was not in tune with its
spirit, and had never troubled to get beyond its
grammar. I was always affected by the look of languages. French, in print, looked to me like barbed
wire, and sounded like somebody wearing very tight
pince-nez, just as German looked like a distant prospect
of astigmatism and sounded like somebody eating
granite, and Scotch looked like somebody trying to
write English with a hare-lip. My choice was Italian.
We had on our mantelshelf two cups of very thin
fluted porcelain, and the sound given by those cups
when struck seemed to me just like the look of printed
Italian. Ever since then, reading Italian, even a
leading article in the *Corriere della Sera*, has always
seemed to me like reading honeysuckle and cream.

Anyway, with the help of three or four Ollendorf
phrases I crossed the river at Rouen and found my
other station and got to Vernon. And there, one
night, I slipped again into real life. There was midsummer midnight ; an unlit room with window open
to the lane and a full moon giving light to half the room
and leaving the other in luminous shadow. Out of
this shadow a booming monotonous voice was floating in a monologue which held my ears as the moonlight held my eyes.

" . . . so I put my arm under him and raised him
to the pillow. His forehead was beaded with sweat.
I thought he was going to speak. But he didn't.
Then he looked as though he was about to cough. But
he didn't cough. His mouth opened and he gasped.
Then the head fell sideways. I put my hand to his
heart and felt no beat. The poet was dead."

I saw the little bedroom, and the thin face and figure
whose portrait I knew ; and I saw my host's large
figure bent over it in feminine tenderness, and I saw
his arm sliding beneath the poet to raise him. And

I saw the poet lying back on the pillow with his head
on one side, and I saw my host's hand on his heart.

Since eleven o'clock he had been talking, my Author,
of his friends and acquaintances of the past, of Daudet
and Zola, of De Maupassant, Oscar Wilde, Verlaine ;
and then of the poet who had died in his arms. The
voice went on and on.

" . . . I hadn't seen him for some time. Then,
just before Christmas of that year I happened to go
into the ' Bodega.'   The Bedford Street ' Bodega.'
And I saw him at a table. He was drinking gin. He
was shivering. And when I shook hands with him I
found his hand burning hot. I said, ' Ernest, you're
ill.' He said it was nothing and didn't matter. And
with him it didn't. All the time I knew him he wanted
to die. I asked who was looking after him and he
said Nobody. I was in low circumstances myself just
then. I was living in rooms in the suburbs—at Catford. But I saw he couldn't be left alone as he was,
so I suggested he come home with me, and let my landlady look after him. At first he wouldn't hear of it.
But he was so apathetic that I easily overruled him.
So I took him home with me to Catford. To die in
Catford—quite near where he was born."

I was looking out to the moonlit lane, but I didn't
see it. Where the lane was I saw Bedford Street,
and I saw my Author leading a wasted poet down it
and along the Strand to Charing Cross, and I saw
them in the train, and I saw them getting out at
Catford.

" . . . and he stayed with me for some weeks, and
I saw him fading every day. He should have been in
the South but neither of us had any money. Then
one night he sat talking for hours. Talking, talking,
talking. Of all manner of things. I never heard him
talk so much. Quite strange things for him. He
wanted to read Dickens—the whole of Dickens. A
writer he'd always shrunk from. He'd done no work
while he was with me. Not a scrap of writing that I

could see. He seemed withdrawn from all that. The
light had gone out of his face. But that night he
went on talking of plans. Literary plans. I couldn't
get him to go to bed. Perhaps he knew it was the
last night."

The basso boomed out of the shadow where the
Author was only a dim shape, a red bead of cigarette,
and a voice. From where I sat I could just see,
through the pines and poplars, a white glint which was
the Seine, and which gave cool tone to the hot stillness. I remember thinking there was nothing very
" foreign " about that river, as I had foolishly expected.
That visit was my first sight of foreign soil and a foreign
river, and it had not brought the special excitement
I felt was due from it. At Dieppe I had seen nothing
much more " foreign " than at Newhaven. The
public notices were different ; the trains were a little
different ; the costume of the porters was different.
But only different ; not at all " foreign."

It was not until I reached Rouen that I was really
aware that I had broken connexion with England ;
and then it was nothing about the city itself, or its
buildings, its shops, the dress of its people or its tram-
cars, or the French-town smell of coffee and rank
cigarettes that did it. None of those things gave me
the stab of strangeness. But just by the rue Jeanne
d'Arc was a line of cafés, and it was there that I received my first sensation of Abroad. In the whole
moving scene of Rouen in early morning sunshine one
thing stood out to my eye ; one thing cried Foreign
Country. It was the sight of a road-sweeper sitting
outside one of the cafés—drinking claret.

With long pauses the narrative of the poet's last
night went on, the tones reverberating round the little
room and floating out to the lane ; and in that story
of the passing of an English minor poet in a London
suburb, told in that place and in those circumstances,
I felt life coming alive and the summer night coming
alive, and Vernon and France and everything. The

City office where I drudged all day with the sense of having my right foot in a left boot, and to which I would have to go back, was an ugly shadow of a sham world. That midsummer midnight was real. I knew that it was a night I would always remember. The night itself, silver velvet in quality, was an occasion ; and that contact with my first Author, and through him with poets and novelists before whose work I bowed, and his choice of that dramatic hour at which to tell his dramatic story, heightened the occasion to the power of a presence.

I could illuminate and embroider what he was say- ing. At sixteen I had read much of the splendours and miseries of the poets ; of the short lives and squalid ends of the Bankside poets, and of the wretched stories of Chatterton and of Dermody, of Mangan and Poe and of De Nerval (hanged on a lamp-post out- side a brothel) and of Murger and Verlaine and others. That night I was brought close to the end of almost the last of the luckless line, whose miserable passing in the last year of the nineteenth century marked the passing not only of the misery of poets but also, it seems now, of their splendour. I had taken the hand of my Author, and he had taken *his* hand, so there was a faint contact ; and as the narrative went on I could see the poet and hear his speech, and could feel his mishaps and his heartbreaks over his Adelaide, and his forlorn evasions of life and his aimless days, and his end in that characterless suburb.

" . . . but at last I was able to get him to bed. He had an attack of coughing and a series of spasms. I had quite a job with him. I had to lift him into bed."

I saw that five-room villa in a Catford street of a hundred similar villas. I saw the highly individual poet dying in one of those hundred villas as unmarked from the other ninety-nine as one soldier from another in a parade of flesh or lead soldiers. I saw the broken Ernest being lifted into bed.

" . . . it was some time before he slept, but about

four o'clock he went off. Next morning I saw he was much worse. I saw the end was near. I wired to his nearest relative—*Ernest in extremis. Come.* But the wire was too late."

And then came the description of the last minute. The voice boomed on and on as though it had been talking through centuries of nights. As indeed it had. It had all happened before. That white midnight was only one of millions, repeated and repeated through the ages. All through the ages poets had died in poverty in back bedrooms in poor streets, or in hospitals, and their friends had recounted their endings. All through the ages young and ardent creatures had struggled on this star with the mystery of life, and some of them had made the service of beauty a faith for which they sacrificed all except their integrity, without knowing the nature of that beauty or the nature of themselves or the nature of anything. While the shrewd and prudent had watched them in pity and disgust at their folly.

It was all happening in one long moment. All those things that had taken centuries of time in their happening, all the lives of those dead poets which had taken years in the actual living, were compassed by my mind in a few seconds of thought. Thought, I saw, could embrace everything. In the physical we were bound to time and place, but in thought we could range and bring all things into one immediate moment. In thought we could live in ten different worlds in a flash. We could hold a conversation with a friend, and watch something going on across the street, and think of the letter we would be writing, and of the letter Horace Walpole or somebody wrote, and think of what we will have for lunch, and re-hear the last performance of the *Eroica*, all in one moment.

And I saw that all those tragic lives and those pitiful deaths of poets bearing different names were all one ; one recurrent figure in a pattern. It was one moon shining in one night and one poet dying one

death.   For the struggling creatures on this star there
is no end, no break or pause.   The stars dance through
space, and things change their form, and the dance
goes on in hope and despair, grief and joy, parting
and meeting, swift and slow, and none of it is separate
to itself ;   only aspects of one pattern in one arrested
moment.

.   .   .   .   .   .

It was during that summer that I had my first
dazzling experience of opera, and it was fitting, after
those Vernon nights of talk about the hapless poets
of London and Paris, that by accident my first opera
should have been the opera based on that novel which
is their justification and apology.

There, in the opera-house of Covent Garden, I again
found life.   There, artificial as the setting might be,
there, in those hours of music and song, was truth.
Those gallery nights were not nights of mere pleasure ;
they were nights of intense living, and among my
lantern-slides of memory they are the most clearly
focused.   No outer turmoil can take our memories
away.   They remain always at call, and we can evoke
them in times of the sorest stress, in any orgy of the
world's dirt, and the events live in all their first shining
felicity.   So with my opera-nights.   Each of them,
separate from the others, I can recall and can hear
that opera and the voices that sang it and that particular evening's experience in all its individual
detail.

Those nights took me into a new world, yet a very
old world.   The stone walls and the drab hoardings
of every day were down, and there was life revealed
in Song ;   Song, man's first art, learned from moun-
tain-stream and forest-wind.   Song is not an expression of something.   It is its own meaning ;   nothing
but Song.   And at Covent Garden there was such
song as I had not then dreamed of.   Those Mediterranean voices of gold and crystal were not voices only ;

they were more than sound issuing from a human throat. As the beam of Sound issued it took a life of its own, and, like a new-born child, it was filled by a spirit that was not of the singer but was part of all life ; and that spirit stole into my nerves and blood and became for ever part of me and of my own being.

I had no judgment or discrimination. Opera was opera, and I ate it. Some of the things then done have never since been done in England. Current taste has frowned upon them, and they lie neglected on the library shelf. No doubt they were poor things ; trite in their libretti and too florid and too sweet in their melodies ; the confectionery of music. But I found them delightful confectionery, and at that time they helped me to make sense of life. Melody is too naïf for modern ears, and probably no young people of to-day would sit through, let alone stand hours for, those slender early-nineteenth-century things of Donizetti and Bellini—*Lucia, La Favorita, Don Pasquale, Norma, I Puritani.* Other now-neglected things I heard were Meyerbeer's *Dinorah, Gli Ugonotti* and *Le Prophète ;* Massenet's *Manon* and *Thais* ; Gluck's *Orfeo ;* Verdi's *Don Carlos, Un Ballo in Maschera* and *La Forza del Destino ;* Boito's *Mefistofele ;* Giordano's *Andrea Chenier* and Cilèa's *Adrienne Lecouvreur.* They were sorted with the standard and still current things of Mozart and Rossini, Verdi, Mascagni and Puccini. All of them gave me immortal hours.

The very names of the singers made for me a ringing rainbow of song across the heavy London scene —Destinn, Scotti, Journet, Marcoux, Sammarco, Giachetti, Donalda, van Rooy, Maurel, and the king and queen of them all, Caruso and Melba. Even the names of the conductors—Mancinelli, Campanini, Mugnone—carried song. The price exacted for those immortal hours I gladly paid. To get a night of opera and the price of a gallery-seat meant going without a mid-day meal for four days. On days when this abstinence had produced almost the necessary half-

I

crown, and I was able to hear an opera, I was only able to complete the half-crown by having no meal that day but breakfast, and nothing till next morning except a penny bar of milk-chocolate eaten at the gallery door during the two-hour wait.

During the wait an Italian with an accordion would prepare us for our evening with selections from opera's rough young brothers of the street—those Neapolitan songs which, spun out of a southern sun and sea, have gone throbbing round the world and fixed themselves in the hearts of millions who know nothing of the scenes or occasions upon which they were made. Banal, perhaps, but immortal. Their very titles are song—*Torni à Sorrento* . . . *Santa Lucia* . . . *T'm'arricordo a Napole* . . . *O sole mio* . . . *Funiculi, funicula* . . . *Mamma mia* . . . *Cielo turchino.* No Englishman can sing them. The English voice cannot yell with the passion or howl with the yearning of those airs. No English singer, however shrewd an actor, can strip himself of his blood-birthright of reserve and his fear of making himself ridiculous, and let himself go in the naked abandon which is the Neapolitan nature in song. Our Italian entertainer could, and made Floral Street vibrate with his passion.

And then at last the doors would open, and there was the going-in, the settling down, the entry of the orchestra, and the reproduction of the primal mystery of Creation. There was the tuning-up—the Chaos before Order. And then the darkening of the house —the Valley of the Shadow which precedes the Glory. And then the murmuring and throbbing of the music of the Spheres. And then the Rending of the Veil, and the disclosure of Light and the whole realm of Song.

From some of those nights, especially the nights when the new tenor, Enrico Caruso, had sung, I walked home, or staggered home, through the sultry night physically exhausted with emotional tension and want of food, but morally exhilarated beyond any sense of physical fatigue. Those poignant Mediterranean arias and those voices from the blue coasts had the same effect as certain magic lines of verse ; they transmuted all the everyday things and illuminated all life with a Gloria. And in hours when the grind of my lifeless, friendless City days reduced me sometimes to a pulp of depression, I would recall the passion and nobility of that Caruso voice or the porcelain quality of that Melba voice, and I would say, This life of futile drudgery is a lie. *That's* what life really is.

But those who knew this had to pay for their knowledge by sacrifice. At sixteen my large and miscellaneous reading had covered a good deal of biography, and I knew something of the men who had made that fabric of song, and I saw how they had shared the splendours and miseries of the poets. There were the arias of *Norma* and *La Sonnambula* ; and there was Bellini, the Sicilian Angel, dying alone at thirty-three in a deserted villa, neglected by his host and left in his last agonising hours with no attendant save the gardener. There were the arias of *Don Pasquale* and *Lucia* ; and there was Donizetti returning to Bergamo, his birthplace, to pass his last hours with mind gone and body a wreck. There were the crystal airs of *Figaro* and *Don Giovanni* ; and there was Mozart, at thirty-six almost forgotten, dying in poverty and receiving pauper burial. There was the heroic fire of *Le Damnation de Faust* ; and there was Berlioz, wrestling through life with derision, misunderstanding, failure and heartbreak. Always that marriage of Sorrow and Song ; children of the sun condemned to the shadow. " Behold this dreamer. . . . Let us slay him." At sixteen those things troubled me.

.   .   .   .   .

When in the early part of that year, my first story was accepted, I felt myself on the way to become an author. I had had dreams, arising from Freda, about music, but she had shown me that they were fancies painted on the air; I hadn't got the elements of it.. But the solid achievement of the acceptance of that story when I was sixteen led me to abandon idle fancies and to set all thought and energy in one direction. Very soon, though in my general state I was sure of little, I was sure of one thing; that somehow or other my life would be spent in or around literature; that it would be in the fullest sense devoted to literature.

I thought then that the artist is the manifestation of man at his highest and noblest poise and power. It was, I felt, only by its artists that a country truly lived; they were the source of its inspiration and the expression of its aspiration. One could see that that was true because it was accepted, if unconsciously, by everybody in their thought of the different countries. The name of any particular country brought an echo not of its self-important public men but of its artists. The thought of Italy brought Leonardo and Raphael and Michelangelo; Dante, Petrarch, Cellini and Verdi. Spain meant Cervantes and Calderon, Velasquez, El Greco and Murillo and Goya. England did not evoke the names of traders, ministers or rulers. The styling of certain periods as the Elizabethan Age, Augustan Age, Georgian Age or Victorian Age was a falsity. Elizabeth, Anne, the Georges, Victoria, had nothing to do with the making of the real England. They were concerned only with political affairs—the façade of a country's life. The real life was made by the outstanding spirits of an age.

And rulers do not create these spirits; it is the outstanding spirits who influence and colour the rulers. Elizabeth had nothing to do with making the English Renaissance; the English Renaissance had a lot to do with making Elizabeth. And to-day, to any foreigner, England means Shakespeare, Spenser, Milton and Herrick; Fielding and Johnson; Shelley and Wordsworth and Byron and Dickens; Reynolds

and Constable and Turner ; Purcell and Gibbons and
Arne. Those names are the true soul of England,
and I felt there could be no finer life than to do service
in any small capacity in the purlieus of one of the arts,
and for me the art would be literature. Priggish ?
Very likely. My only friend had always called me the
Funny One, which was perhaps a polite synonym for
the other term, and at sixteen or seventeen few of us
can escape being either lout or prig.

That first accepted story, for which I received one
guinea, was, of course, rubbish ; a magazine story
of the conventional kind. But it had an interesting
genesis. It derived from my ninth year. It was in
that year that the desire to tell a story first came
to me, and the desire had its origin in an odd event
whose setting was a neighbouring suburb ; an event
which not only shook up my interior life at that time,
and awoke a desire to tell tales, but coloured the whole
of my later life.

In that neighbouring suburb lived an aunt who
kept a confectioner's shop, and that year she asked
me to spend Christmas with her. To a child of nine
a Christmas holiday at a confectioner's is in itself a
Christmas present ; in addition I liked the aunt, and
there were the stimulating attendant details of the visit.
There was the pleasure of the little journey by two
buses, and the arrival after dark at a place I had not
then seen. There was the shop, gay and gorgeous with
decorations and with Christmas cakes and pastries.
There was the excitement of a new house and new
rooms with different smells and different things to
look at. There was the excitement of a new bedroom
and a thrill entirely new to my experience—of a fire
in the bedroom. At bedtime there was the bewildering excitement of being allowed to choose from the
shop just one cake from the many trays of cakes and
tarts and puffs ; confections too light and lovely to
be eaten ; gay trinkets of food to be consumed by the
eye and the nose. And in the bedroom, after the light

was out, there was the æsthetic wonder of the play of
firelight on the walls and ceiling, and the harmony
of contrast made by the indoor and outdoor worlds
of fire and snow.

In that room the event happened. I went to sleep
thinking of trays and trays of marvellous cakes, and
of mysterious packages which stood on a small table
near the fire, and which I was put upon my honour
not to touch till the morning. But in the morning
their urgent appeal had lost half its urgency.

During the night I had a dream. I had, I suppose,
dreamt before but without remembering ; I always
awoke fully in the present world. But on that Christmas morning I came back very slowly and reluctantly
to the world. The dream was so intense that when I
woke I was still in it, and the strange bedroom helped
to hold me back from the present ; there was nothing
in it of my everyday. So that some minutes passed
before I fully awoke and realised that the extraordinary scenes in which I had moved, and the extraordinary
happenings I had shared, were all what was called a
dream.

Even when I was up and dressed I was not properly
back in the everyday, and it took me some time to
return to the delightful fact of Christmas Morning.
The opening of presents engaged only half my mind,
and even the excitement of breakfasting by lamplight surrounded by tissued treasures did not detach
me from the event of the night. During the morning
I was silent, and they thought I wasn't well. The
dream still hung about me and called me. It hung
about me all day, hovering insistently on the edge of
consciousness, the full memory of it just out of reach ;
so that three or four times that day I went up to my
bedroom in the hope that as it had happened there, I
might there re-enter it and continue it to its sweet
and terrible climax. But I could catch only its spirit.

It was a dream that I could not, even now, tell
easily to another : it was too fragile and no skill could

make it sound anything but ridiculous, which it wasn't. Its scene was not in England, but it was not outlandish or fantastic ; not Assyria or Cathay or Ethiopia. Its scene was a house, but a house out of any time or place I had ever known or heard of. It was a house of three floors with comfortably furnished rooms on each floor, and the rooms seemed never to have been used and were thus emitting the pure essence of " roomness." But the three floors kept repeating themselves, so that after the third floor I found above it a repetition of the first floor, and so on. I knew both in the dream and on waking that I had never been in any house at all like it, yet I could find my way about it, and I knew what rooms the next staircase led to and their relative positions. All the rooms on each floor had the appearance of having been got ready to receive somebody but had clearly never received anybody. I was alone in the house. There was no sign or sound of any living creature, though there was life enough in the house itself, its walls and its contents. But though I was alone and met no hindrance in my wanderings up and down the stairs and in and out of the rooms, I knew, in the dream, that it was not for me that those rooms were waiting. There was somebody else to come. The rooms didn't resent my intrusion nor did they welcome me. The silence wasn't like the silence of some empty houses—a silence that threatens to rush out of the rooms behind you and suffocate you. It was an aloof silence that took no notice of me. There they were, those rooms, all alive, ears and eyes and spirits at the alert, waiting for that somebody. That was the setting. Then came the series of events, strange and sweet and outside my experience, to which I was a reluctant and fascinated witness.

It was a dream charged with such fervour, in an atmosphere of such spiritual power, that all present things, even Christmas, seemed without lustre. It was such a dream as men have recorded from their traffic with laudanum or hashish, making all the

delights of this earth weary and hollow. Every
feature of it lived in a blaze of light. The scene was
night and darkness, yet the house was illuminated by
a white darkness far brighter than our day, and of its
nature I can only say that it was like nightmare made
pure and enchanting.

As the days passed the details of it grew less keen,
but it never wholly faded, and at this moment I can
see that house and those rooms and their furniture
as clearly as I saw them on that morning's awakening.
I could not, as I say, tell it to anyone, but it aroused
in me the desire to tell *a* story, any story, to tell *something* to other people. And a week or so later, at the
age of nine, I wrote or half-wrote a story that had some
faint relation to the dream. It wasn't, of course, the
dream itself ; that I kept and always have kept hidden.
It was an invention arising out of a minor point of the
dream. I never finished it, and to-day I can recall
nothing of it save its title. That title gives some hint
of the dream, though I don't now know what it meant.
The title was—*The House Behind the Midnight*.

.   .   .   .   .   .

On all events of the past Time throws an autumn
light that whisks away the troubled air in which
they grew and reveals them as they were—vital experience in our development. Nothing that we suffer,
whether of delight or distress, is fully realised at the
time. In all felicitous hours there is a tincture of
pain ; all periods of misery are shot with random
veins of bliss. But only in retrospect do we know
that. Then, in that autumn light, the most painful
and ugly episodes, purged of the cumbering circumstance of their occasion, and surviving only as the
crystallised essence of themselves, take a passionate
quality and an edge of sweetness that brings them
into proportion to the happier episodes and makes
them all one experience.

In my teens I had certain squalors to endure :

loneliness and ungainly surroundings, and those little corroding distresses—shabby clothes, scanty food, exposed ignorance—which wound so much more keenly than heavier afflictions.   Yet those distresses, dark as they were, could throw a thread of silver into the years to come.   They came to me in the morning mist of the climate of youth, when, though mind and nerves may be lacerated, the heart is light ; when even misery can be exhilarating and all seasons, even drab winters, have the stirring quality of springtime, and all occasions, sweet and bitter, make their impact sharply and become shining factors in the sum of life.   And the struggles and adjustments involved in meeting those distresses kept my mind always awake and gave me eyes to see through walls and through human masks. I was in my middle teens, and at that stage if one has not been clouded by a standardised education and the acceptance of conventional codes, one still has the percipience of childhood.

On the surface my life was a life of restricted circumstance, ignobly decent and without event, but accompanied by frequent internal diversion in the form of adventures among books and music and pictures. In my daily life physically alone, I kept a crowded company of the mind, and if the people were not substantial I could content myself with the reflection that most of the people among whom I spent my working day were no more so.   I lived mainly through imagination, reverie, emotion and (occasionally) thought, and the weariness of my days and weeks was crossed by a filigree of things wholly incongruous with my ugly surroundings.   Among those things were English and American literature, Italian opera, literary periodicals, Queen's Hall and Albert Hall and Bechstein Hall concerts, English landscapes in the National Gallery, midnight wanderings through London highways and byways, and the writing of short stories and exercises in verse in the French forms of villanelle, chant-royal, ballade and rondel.

I took to English literature as naturally as to my food. The works I read were all new to me, but never strange. I seemed to know them before I came to know them, and as I received from each work the sting or shock of its quality, it was a familiar sting or shock, as though I had come again among long-forgotten friends. For weeks at a time during those years I lived in a world of new yet recognisable sensations from which mind and nerves received a strength that made them impervious to the blemishes about me. But none of those delights was in itself a full satisfaction. They were no more than keys to life, the real life in which, by the claims of the daily grind at futile monotonous tasks, I could live only for short spells.

By those things only was I sustained in the daily grind. At the back of my mind was a faint hope that some time or other I might escape from it, but it was so faint that it never became a thought. I seemed to be bound for ever to a treadmill where work, work for its own sake, however purposeless, was exalted into a virtue, and where doing nothing was called Wasting Time and was condemned as a sin. That I believed, and still believe, to be a lie, and I arranged with myself that if ever I did manage to escape that treadmill I would for the rest of my life do as little work as possible ; nothing more than was necessary for a modest support. I would never work for the sake of occupation. I would never be what so many men called themselves, not with apology but with pride —a Busy Man. I would use my life mainly for Being and only incidentally for Doing.

Work I saw as an ugly name for an ugly thing ; so ugly that men were moved to justify their worship of the false god by inventing a fable that it had been imposed upon them by divine wrath. By Work, of course, I don't mean agreeable engagement. I mean senseless, ant-like industry, work for the sake of doing something or piling up possessions. Watching that kind of work I turned gratefully to Idleness. Work was barbarous. Idleness was civilised. I knew it in all my nerves. I knew that the right life, the true art of living, lay in that creative indolence enjoyed by Gray and Gilbert White and Landor and Fitz-gerald, an indolence yielding far richer experience than any ant-like industry.

Work, the ugly thing, was the father of many other ugly things. The accepted idea that the active man is virtuous and the indolent man a sinner is a fallacy that has wrought much misery upon us. Another fallacy was tacked to it ; that Satan will always find mischief for idle hands to do ; a fallacy on the face of it, since the hands, being those of an idler, could never, even by Satan, be stirred to action. The truth is the opposite. It is the active and energetic for whom Satan finds mischievous employment ; those who are incapable of Being and must for ever be Doing. It is among them that Satan finds his readiest tools, and the condition of to-day's world is a witness to how well they serve their master. If somebody somehow could seduce all these restless creatures into the opium habit the world would be a quieter and happier place for the many who are concerned with other values than those of power and dominion.

Of all the influences that crossed those days the most stimulating to me, odd as it may seem to those who knew more normal circumstances, were the monthly issues of that now-dead literary magazine, the *Book-man*. I lived through each month for it ; after each issue I was looking impatiently for the next. It was my only peep-hole into my own world—the world where I was at home, and from which, by my lack of this and that, I was as cut off as if that world were beyond the moon. In its gossip, its reviews, its por-traits and other illustrations, its studies of the figures of English literature, and its publishers' advertise-ments, it was my Magic Lantern. I still keep a file of it, or at least several years' run of the old thing, and I have only to pick up any issue of it—say November 1902 or April 1903—and up comes, as with the old music-hall songs, a whole caravan of associations warm and bright as in the moment of their experience. I need only look at the cover, and I know at once on what evening or morning I bought it, and what the weather was, what the events of the time, what was happening in the unquiet corners of my mind, what books I was reading, what story I was trying to write. It serves as a mnemonic system that works back and forth. If in talk or reading I come to a reference to March 1903, my mind throws up the Lamb number of the *Bookman*, which throws up twenty other matters ; a reference to July 1904 throws up the Hawthorne number and a stifling summer evening ; and a reference to October 1904 throws up the Brontë number, and tea and toast in the aromatic atmosphere of a Ye Mecca Café, and a misty and spangled evening.

I bought regularly many other literary periodicals of a light kind—the *Literary World*, *Great Thoughts*, the *Academy*, *T.P.'s Weekly*, the *Book Monthly*, but none of them made the intimate personal appeal to me of the *Bookman*. But the *Bookman* I bought wasn't of course quite the magazine that other people bought. It was something produced in answer to an unspoken prayer of mine ; it was exactly the periodical I needed and was charged for me with something more than articles and pictures concerning books and writers. Other people bought a popular literary magazine which they read with critical detachment and compared with more serious organs ; I bought a Magic Lantern. The buying of each issue carried its own peculiar thrill on which hung a number of minor thrills. There was the feel of its leaves ; the glance at the cover to see to which figure of English literature that month's number was devoted ; the temptation to take peeps into its pages while walking home, and the resistance of the temptation so that all the thrill of its contents should be received fresh and full in the quiet of home or, if I had the necessary pence, in the corner of a Ye Mecca ; and the knowledge that when one got home or got to the tea-shop there would be a rich hour which would somehow work back and suffuse all the preceding hours of the day with its richness and make it, whatever it had been, a day of purring content.

The decoration, at that time, of my bedroom was as incongruous as that of most boys' bedrooms. On the wall at the bed's head were presentation plates from the *Bookman* of Lamb, Keats, Shelley, Coleridge, Milton, Fitzgerald, Blake and Goethe ; and portraits cut from other periodicals of Spenser, Sidney, Herrick, Waller, Marvell and Cowley. On the wall at the side were portraits of Handel, Bach, Mozart, Beethoven, Schubert, Berlioz, Schumann and Verdi. Elsewhere were portraits of Thomas Browne, De Quincey, Gertie Millar, Poe, Swinburne, Heine, Meredith, Clarence Mangan, Hawthorne, Caruso, Oscar Wilde, Marie Studholme, Baudelaire, George Gissing, Stephen Crane, Matthew Arnold and Zena Dare.

My library was composed of volumes of the cheaper reprints—the Canterbury Poets, the Scott Library, World's Classics, and one or two of George Newnes' Thin Paper Classics. Each volume had meant the missing of at least two meals ; the George Newnes' volumes, being more expensive, had meant four missed meals. There were also a few rakings from Paternoster Row and Farringdon Road, paid for by walking home from the City, four miles, instead of taking bus or tram.

I made those small but cutting sacrifices with, I fear, very little grace and with weak and aching limbs. I never used bad language, but in moments when life was intolerable I often thought it and developed a habit of mental swearing. Usually on those homeward trudges I swore myself home. But at various points of London I would remember that there had been ardent spirits who had known far more distresses than mine and in sharper degree. Passing Brook Street,

Holborn, I would remember the young and ardent spirit who had suffered so much more in 1770 than a mere nobody was suffering in 1903. In Clerkenwell I would recall Johnson's Grub Street days, and passing the Temple I would remember Lamb and his hated servitude to the desk's dead wood, and in Covent Garden I would recall Dermody's last days, and at Hungerford Bridge the bleak days of young Dickens in the blacking factory, and I would forget my own hunger and weakness and other distresses in youthful indignation at theirs.

My special treasures among my books were the Newnes' Thin Paper Classics. The format and binding of that series were designed by Granville Fell, and each volume had a frontispiece portrait on Japan paper by Edmund Sullivan and a title-page on Japan paper designed by Garth Jones. They were the earliest books to be issued on the then-new India paper, and you could get the whole of Lamb in one volume, all Hawthorne's novels in one volume, Peacock's novels in one volume, and the whole of Milton, Burns, Evelyn's *Diary*, Coleridge, Marlowe, each in one volume of foolscap 8vo., some of the volumes running to nearly eight hundred pages, and none of them of greater thickness than half an inch.

Of the prose authors whose works I bought in one or other of the reprint series my preferences were Sir Thomas Browne, Cowley, Landor, Heine, Poe, De Quincey, Hazlitt, Hawthorne, Washington Irving, Matthew Arnold and Peacock. I have tried in later years to perceive in those disparate authors some common denominator, some inter-relation, that could lead a boy of sixteen in his individual taste and judgment to make an allied company of them, but I can see none. There they were, on a special shelf by my bed, and there, in my present bookcases, some of them still are. My choice took in none of early youth's ordinary stuff—no Carlyle or Ruskin or Emerson, no Addison or Macaulay, no Scott or Stevenson ; no

philosophy or science, no political history. I looked
at those things, and took them up, and my fingers
told me they were not my books. Of modern authors
of the period I read Oscar Wilde, Arthur Symons,
Quiller-Couch, James Lane Allen, George Gissing,
Andrew Lang, Zangwill, George Moore, Kipling and
Stephen Crane. The last was an important discovery ;
a vivid lesson to me in descriptive writing and a lasting
influence. Having found one book of his, *George's
Mother*, which gave me a shock of illumination into
the mystery of writing, I sought out all he had done,
and in quick succession read *Maggie*, *The Red Badge
of Courage*, and the volumes of stories and sketches,
The Open Boat, *The Monster*, *The Little Regiment*,
Last Words, and *Wounds in the Rain*. Each volume
was an awakening to a new sense of the shape and hue
of words and the structure of a sentence. His quiver-
ing sensibility, the sword-flash of his style, and the
ice-gleam of his observation were qualities I had not
found in any of our own writers of the time, and they
were present in every little magazine article or fugitive
story that I was able to dig up. And there was the
arresting stab of his openings. Not even Kipling was
more direct and vivid :

A baby was wandering in a strange country.

*They were youths of subtle mind. They were very
wicked according to report and yet they managed to
have it reflect great credit upon them.*

*The cold passed reluctantly from the earth and the
retiring fogs revealed an army stretched out on the hills,
resting.*

*A very little boy stood upon a heap of gravel for the
honour of Rum Alley. He was throwing stones at
howling urchins from Devil's Row . . . .*

None of them knew the colour of the sky.

Here was something that came home to me. It came
home to me in the first two pages of *George's Mother*
with the force of a revelation. That, clearly, was the

way to do it. It was the example and the spur I had
been waiting for, and for long afterwards Stephen
Crane was the measure against which I set all my
inept exercises.

I noted in those pinched days the reaction of one's
physical state to certain books. When weak with
hunger I found it impossible to read novels or essays
of rarefied style or austere thought. I could not
after twenty-four hours without food read Pater or
Matthew Arnold or Meredith or Henry James or
Wilde, or any of the cool and critical and aloof. I
could read only the more earthy and genial and everyday. Those others were agreeable only when the
stomach and nerves were soothed. With music it
was different. I could go to a concert in an enforced
fast and receive the music much more keenly.

Each of my concerts was an adventure that shook
me to death and into new life. In literature I instinctively knew my way about, but in music I was still
in the exploring and undiscriminating stage. Often
I was bewildered, but it was the bewilderment not of
dark but of light. All that I heard deeply moved me,
but I was far from understanding it. But on that
point I encouraged myself with a story I had heard
about Wagner. When he was in England he stayed
with a family in which were two small children. One
afternoon, when they were alone with him in the
drawing-room he went to the piano and played passages from *Tannhäuser* and *Lohengrin*. When he had
done he turned to them and asked, " Did you like
that ? " With the honesty of children they said,
" No," and received the admonition, " Then listen
till you do."

The concert halls of those opening years of the century were much occupied by infant prodigies of violin
and piano. The infant prodigy is to-day out of
fashion, but at that time we had Franz von Vecsey,
Florizel von Reuter, Vivien Chartres, Mischa Elman,
Elsie and Vernon Warner, and others whom I have

forgotten. I heard all of them, and my admiration
was as keen as my hopeless wish that I could be like
them. The fashionable adult king of the violin just
then was Kubelik. Joachim and Sarasate could still
be heard, but the young newcomer was then receiving
all the incense. Solo musicians *were* kings in those
days ; more than kings, indeed ; they were gods,
almost on the heights of to-day's film performers.
After recitals by Kubelik or Paderewski or Pachmann
I have seen crowds of women waiting at the artists'
entrance, and when the god came out they would surge
upon him and mob him, satisfied if they might just
touch the hem of the god's overcoat.

My life in those City years was, as I say, mainly
cloud but shot with many lightning flashes of sharp
content. If I lived in material want I lived also in
mental luxury, so that when the material want became
clamant, as it often did, I would remind myself of a
music-hall song of the time—*MUST You Have Beef
with your Mustard?* What deepened the cloud was
that I had nothing to look forward to, no assured
hope that my faint dream of something more seemly
and sensible would ever take form. I could not
accept those old wives' tales that everything comes
right in the end. I wanted to know what end—when ?
If that consummation were set in a futurity of forty
million years, the tale might be true. But the history
of the world, so far as it has gone, shows that things
only go right for a time, that right conquers only for
a time ; that truth prevails only for a time ; and then
comes the reversion to wrong.

So, as I could see nothing before me, I began, even
at sixteen and seventeen, to look back. There was
no repetition of my visit to France and the faint
contact it gave with the world of letters. I heard
occasionally from my Author, but only occasionally ;
and for the rest I lived friendless with no means of
sharing either my miseries or joys. Freda had gone
to Paris at thirteen, just as the Boer War began, and

when all street-organs were playing *The Absent-Minded Beggar*, and she was still there. I had, at the beginning, a few letters from her, at first full of excited anticipation, and then saying that her Professor was a slave-driver who was killing her; that she had to work much harder than she had expected, though of course she had expected she would; that she was seeing nothing of Paris and getting no fun, and was often too tired in the evening to write a letter. After a few months the letters dwindled and finally died, and she became first a memory, and later not even as imponderable as that; nothing more than a faint echo of something I had once remembered.

I had a feeling that I would never see her again, and I wasn't sure whether I wanted to. I had grown accustomed to living without friends. When she had first gone I had been sensible of a dull ache, but with the end of the perfunctory correspondence the ache had eased, the gap made by her going had closed and had become part of my general loneliness, and was no longer perceived. To meet her again might be embarrassing to both of us. She might no longer be Freda. She might be like all other grown-up young girls as I had observed them—shrill and egotistical and expecting admiration.

Besides, it wasn't always easy to resume a broken acquaintance, even if you wanted to. We might have grown out of each other. Certainly she, I felt, after a life in Paris, must have grown out of me. With my youthful illusions about Paris I imagined she would have become hard and worldly, detached from her old home associations and contemptuous of them. I myself, by the time I was nineteen, became, like most youths, a little ashamed of my early enthusiasms; a little ashamed of having ever felt as I had about a music-hall acrobat, of ever having been moved by crude street-songs and by second-rate books, and by her childish piano-playing. I became a little ashamed of having found such burning delight in Donizetti and

Verdi and Puccini, and having been so excited by the
Bookman, and having found that commonplace suburb
so picturesque and pleasing. It was not until some
years later that I realised that these things, tame as
perhaps they were, had given me sustenance, had
shone upon my spirit and helped it to grow, and that
however others might shrug at them, I must cherish
them. They must never lightly be dismissed by
me.

But at nineteen, in the false shame of gawky youth,
I felt that all that delight was evidence of mean and
restricted experience which nobody would wish to
confess to, and though at seventeen I had not reached
that state I felt that Freda would have reached it.
Tam-o'-shanters and *Two Little Girls in Blue* she
would no doubt regard as belonging to museums. If
I did see her again our meeting would probably have
no stronger charge than that of polite formality. We
would engage in an antiphony of Do-You-Remember
that had no spirit or real concern in it ; mere words
expecting no response. We would realise that we
had nothing in common beyond memories.

So I thought it better that it should die. And it
did. I never did see her again. She passed out of
my life as a red dot in the grey distance of Geneva
Street, and for some years, as I say, was scarcely a
memory.

But other things, things of even earlier years, were
still with me ; much more with me than the immediacy
of my days among the sleep-walkers of the City. I
could not get away from London even for a short
week-end. I had no friends in the country and no
money for rail-fares nor for the very simplest accom-
modation. For six years, save for that trip to Vernon,
I never saw the country ; I sweltered through six
successive London summers which, in most of those
years, really were sweltering. And all the time I had
a passion for travel. Since I couldn't gratify it I
made it vicariously. I took to hanging about the

London stations watching trains go off to places that
were just names on the map. I watched the Con-
tinental evening train go out, and thought of Vernon.
I collected all sorts of pamphlets from Thomas Cook—
itineraries and descriptions of English and European
travel. I read all the volumes of the Highways and
Byways series, and all Charles Harper's histories of
the English roads and James Hissey's English tours.

For the rest I lived on memories. As Kate Greenaway, during her Hoxton childhood, had had blessed
escapes into a Nottinghamshire village—the scene
of the picture I was going to buy—so I, between eight
and ten, had had escapes into a remote corner of
Hertfordshire, and through burning Julys and Augusts
in Fenchurch Street and Cheapside I would recall its
lanes and meadows and river-walks. I could not
catch again from flowers the life I caught when I was
five. The winds of the world were closing the doors
of extra perception through which I had then lived.
But thought of growing flowers could still give me an
illumination that was one shade beyond the illumination given by verse and music.

The corner of Hertfordshire I knew when I was nine
was not only completely rural ; it was rural in a way
that was not of the 'nineties but of forty or fifty years
earlier. So that I had wandered among Birket Foster
landscapes and met people and children dressed in
the fashions worn by the figures in his drawings. The
talk of the people had been quite alien to me. It was
not that their words were rustic but that they used
unfamiliar constructions. As the landscapes and
costumes were fifty years behind the time, so they
themselves were a hundred years behind. They were
indeed of the eighteenth century, and it was only
later that my reading of eighteenth-century novels
and plays showed me that they had talked to me in
eighteenth-century turns of speech.

Few of the adult workers could read or write, but
most of them were intelligent in the real knowledge

that comes from close contact with the earth. All of them had that abrupt stern courtesy which disconcerts the townsman accustomed to softer modes, and yet surpasses the town's good manners because it comes from the primitive relation of man to man. They were not clods, but they were without any expression of gentle emotion. They helped each other in trouble, but they gave no verbal sympathy and no outward display of the warm heart.

But it was not the people that so much won my affection as Hertfordshire itself and the spirit that moved in it; Hertfordshire with its lonely lanes where at that time nobody passed but the villagers—lanes with unrifled banks of wild flowers of all kinds and colours. Hertfordshire with its stretching and sloping meadows in the late afternoon sun; the odour of the cows coming in at milking-time; the scent of wood-smoke and of mint and clover; the pealing of the bells at twilight from the town a mile away stirring memories of things I knew but had never experienced. There were the long still nights, and the sound of night, which was and yet wasn't a sound; a sort of whisper of silence. And there were the long mornings. There was the sun on the bedroom curtains announcing that the morning was outside waiting for me, and there was the plunge into the wide bare early light, where you seemed to stand in the middle of the world in air as fresh to the throat as cold water, and where light seemed to move in the breeze and to be shed from the grass and tree and river, and all things were visibly living; and all that life flowed into you and became part of you.

But it is not possible for us to pass to another the quality of an enchanted hour. It is made of so many elements—the occasion itself, the situation, the cir-cumstances, the momentary colour of a sky or curve of a tree, the look on a particular face, the scent carried on a moment's wind, and a hundred other attendant details, each a feature of the spiritual presence pervading that particular time and never again to make that happy concourse.

In the lanes and woods of that corner the world was mine. I could run for a mile through a lane or prowl for hours about a wood, and never meet anything but a rabbit or a squirrel, or butterflies brown and gold and tiny moths of mauve and violet. That corner was in the east of the county, the flat pastoral region near the Essex border, and it held the gentle feeling of all pastoral country. It was a friendly country which, unlike downs and mountains, needed man and welcomed him, and as it was my first country it became a standard by which ever since I have measured all country.

When there was nothing else to remember there was always the Dream, the Dream in the room over the confectioner's, riding on my mind in twenty different interpretations and trying to get itself made into a story. It did not, nor has it ever taken form as a story. Yet something of it pervades the idea or the narrative method of some half-dozen of my stories. It went with me in all my labyrinthine London wanderings east and west and north, through those clotted nights of summer or through dirty Saturday afternoons of autumn, when all the features of the streets smelt brown and bad, and through freezing green dusks of winter. It was during the wanderings in the east that it became most pregnant with a progeny of possible stories ; though it was long before those embryos took firm shape. I couldn't have written those stories then. They were there, all around me, at every corner, radiating from the Dream, but I was only aware of them ; nothing more.

In certain lost areas of London at that time, in streets away from its harmonious thunder, the silence and the darkness had a curious quality of portent. The darkness was a darkness without motion or trepidation ; without, it seemed, any life. It squatted on the streets like a shapeless substance, holding its

breath and brooding; a substance that was itself
inert but that cloaked all manner of nervous life and
unperceived eyes and invisible lips whispering half-
made words. That powerful silence of the London
night was full of stories, but I couldn't take them.
I would loiter in those hapless streets while the night
melted away, and I could hear them and feel them
and be quite incompetent to make them my own. I
felt like a teacher of elocution with a hare-lip.

I thought, in the foolish solemnity of sixteen, that
before I wrote them I would need to know something
I didn't then know. I couldn't have named that
something but I knew what it was. It was what
Caruso knew when he was singing, what Poe knew
when he was writing *For Annie*, what Silvario knew
when he was swimming through the air, what Wagner
knew when he was writing Siegfried's Funeral March
in *Die Götterdämmerung*; what De Quincey knew
when he was gliding through London byways under
a dose of laudanum. That was what I wanted to
know, so that I might fuse that knowledge with my
Dream for the making of those half-perceived stories.
But I never did know, and in the event they had to
be made without it.

And I went on living my City days on the thin food
of memories and the frail support of dreams. One
of those dreams was built around a mental love-affair.
It was a love-affair with a girl I had never spoken to
and had not even seen—a young actress whose photo
I had seen outside a Strand theatre. I was so much
caught by that photo that I would actually make
special journeys to the Strand merely to pass that
theatre and look at that photo. I came to see in that
face all that the seventeenth-century lyrists had
poured into their verses of April and May and morning
fields and flowers. It became a part of the scenery
of my life, a beautiful Idea which I never really wished
to materialise. It lived with me in the office and in
the streets and in my home. Waking and sleeping

it was always with me. It was in the sun and the
rain and in all the music I heard and in all the books
I read.

A hundred imaginary sweet episodes I built around
the original of that photo. As a spectator of the affair
I could laugh at myself, yet I continued mentally to
develop it and to devise impossible means of meeting
her. I made numbers of verses to her. I set my
life around her, and made her its standard by which
I tested my conduct. In all my hours she, the unknown, was there, not as a comforting presence, only
as an aching absence.

But it taught me, that imaginary affair, that just
as the sharp shadow on a white wall of a flower, a
man's head, a cat, or any other object, gives more of
the inner reality of the object than the material object
itself, so in love the shadow of unattainable love is
nearer to the reality of love than its actual attainment.
It taught me too the useful lesson that one can live
as intensely in grief as in joy. Either state sharpens
the sensibilities and makes life a vital minute-by-
minute phenomenon.

That period was a brief period of theatre enthusiasm—an enthusiasm that has never since visited me.
London then had four inner-suburban theatres, and it
was the custom for West End companies to visit them
as the start of a provincial tour ; and for a year or two,
whenever I could afford it, I had evenings at the theatre
nearest to my suburb. Those were the days of the
actor-manager, and to that little theatre came Wilson
Barrett with *The Silver King*, Forbes-Robertson with
Mice and Men and *The Light that Failed*, Herbert
Tree with *Resurrection*. The Kendals brought their
repertory—*The Elder Miss Blossom, A Scrap of Paper,
Still Waters Run Deep*. Martin-Harvey gave us *The
Only Way, A Cigarette Maker's Romance* and *The
Breed of the Treshams*. Sir John Hare brought *A
Pair of Spectacles*. Mrs Lewis Waller came with *Zaza*
and Olga Nethersole with *Sapho*. William Gillette

brought *Sherlock Holmes*, H. V. Esmond brought *When We were Twenty-one*, and E. S. Willard *The Cardinal*. Julia Neilson and Fred Terry brought *Sweet Nell of Old Drury* and *The Scarlet Pimpernel*, and George Alexander brought *If I Were King*. Other plays that I saw at that theatre were certain old melodramas—*Two Little Vagabonds*, *The Fatal Wedding*, *The Still Alarm*, *The Broken Melody*, *While London Sleeps*. Rough stuff or, as they say now, ham, but right York or Bradenham ham ; the very stuff of the theatre.

A curious point about that theatre enthusiasm is that while I recall every opera I ever heard, and every singer in those operas, I have of the theatre no memory save the titles of the plays and the names of the chief players. Nothing whatever of the plays themselves, or of the impression made by the players, remains. Irving I could have seen but did not see. I don't know why I abstained from seeing the High Priest of the theatre. Possibly I was put off by a remark I read at that time, made by (I think) Charles Whibley —that the audience at an Irving performance was so rapt and devout that an unscrupulous person could easily have gone round with the plate and taken up quite a collection.

Of all my dreams the most foolish and longest-lived was that of escape from my Bridge of Sighs into a life of more comeliness and sense. London Bridge, not Waterloo, was my Bridge of Sighs. Even to-day, when I see the morning and evening procession across that bridge, I feel that the name is apt. Waterloo I often crossed with delight, for the view it afforded on the west and because it led to the Strand. Oxford Street, unfriendly as it was to De Quincey, was another delight. It was human and bright, and if it was a business street its business was the business of pleasure, and it was filled by people who were not grasping money but spending it. My own stony-hearted step-mother, far more deserving of the name, was the City,

thronged from ten o'clock to six o'clock by a standardised and sterilised life ; men with sunless eyes clutching
and controlling, and going through motions that had
become so much a part of their clockwork natures
that, old as they were, they couldn't stop for fear of
running down. All of them, bankers, speculators,
directors, and their clerks—all On the Make, turning
the wealthiest square mile of England into a square
mile of frigid faces.

The spectacle, even as a spectacle, was to me, in
my mood of priggish intolerance, altogether pathetic.
There must, I felt, be more in life than that. Indeed,
I knew there was. But I could not then know that
those rushing crowds felt it. They all seemed to
approve external activity as a basic law of being, and
to be surprisingly content in signing contracts, writing
figures in ledgers, telephoning, interviewing, dashing
up and down Cornhill and Threadneedle Street,
struggling, planning, intriguing, grubbing up thousands
and using them not for beautiful living or for making
things but for the breeding of more thousands ; and
appearing to think that in all this they were doing
something serious. When I questioned it with one
or two people in the office I was told I was too young
to understand. But there was, I was sure, more
meaning to life than that. Those who knew—the
poets, the painters, the musicians—had said so, clearly
and with authority. Yet none of those people seemed
to recognise it. All those Busy Men, rich and poor,
seemed to agree that life meant facts, which are the
enemies of truth, and facts meant external activity
devoted to acquiring possessions.

As the years crawled on I wanted to die. I contemplated a long continuation of those arid days, and
I contemplated death, and found it preferable. I
lived with the idea of it and found nothing repellent
in the idea of extinction as compared with the idea
of a lifetime among those people. In later years
friends have told me that after recovering from 'flu

they came to a period of intense depression in which they felt quite suicidal. They have asked whether I found the same condition after recovering from 'flu. My answer has been that probably I did but that I had been so used to it in my City days that I wouldn't have noticed it.

But at last, when I was nineteen, the faint hope became fact. I escaped. On a certain Spring morning, when the street-organs were playing *La Maxixe*, and the Green was a great space of bustling wind and good-humoured sun, and the streets of the City were intolerably ill-humoured, I remembered something. I remembered a story about a man who had languished many years in prison until one day a bright idea occurred to him. He got up and tried the door. It was unlocked and he walked out. So with me. Figuratively I tried my door and found it open. Physically in a fit of exasperation I swore at the head clerk, took my hat, and walked out of the office for ever.

Out in the street I realised that at last I was free. I knew too that in the whole world I possessed one and fourpence. But the fact was unreal. All that was real was that I was free. No more going into those bald streets each morning and moving back each evening like a shuttle. No more turning out at eight o'clock into sour mornings of January to perform futile tasks. No more dragging over the Bridge of Sighs under the tantalising sun. No more surrender of my days and hours to the chains of other people. All my time at the command of my own whim. Free to get up when I would ; to lie in bed if I would. Free to go out when I would and come in when I would ; free to see the human western streets and shops in daytime, and attend afternoon concerts, and wander round bookshops, and walk out to the London country, and visit the galleries, and discover new corners of London in their morning life. Able, now I was free, to discard all foolish daydreams and all querulous concern about myself and my affairs, and to begin the business of living.

Free. . . . It seemed the most inexhaustible gift one could receive, and the fact that I had no money and no prospect of next week's food beyond the possible continuance of my intermittent luck with stories and articles, took no edge from the joy of the gift. I was free ; and better the thinnest of blankets in the attics of freedom than thousands a year at the cost of surrendered hours.

CHAPTER IX

FREE LANCE

" ANYBODY," said George Gissing, "who encourages any young man or woman to look for his living to literature, commits no less than a crime."

At sixteen I had settled, as I say, that my career, or more accurately, as it turned out, my saunter or series of lurches, would lie in literary work. But when I was eighteen, and had given myself the freedom of the street, and was looking to literature as my only means of support, the few literary men I had met all corroborated George Gissing and sounded the alarm. None of them committed Gissing's " crime." My author in France, Robert Sherard, warned me. Wilfred Whitten warned me. A literary agent warned me. Jack London, with whom I had some correspondence, sent me a warning from California. Morley Roberts warned me. They used the words " precarious," " edge of a precipice," " bitter struggle," " nerve-racking," in relation to the literary life as a sole source of income ; and their warnings were as effective as most warnings from elder to young.

They were of course right, but they didn't know that the very terms they used to intimidate and dissuade

me were so many encouragements. I had already
learned that only when we are in danger are we fully
alive. Security had no attractions for me. Safety
First I considered a motto for neurotics. Success, even
earning a living, would have to look after themselves.
I had none of the anxious preoccupation of some young
men with the future. I had no desire to " win "; no
desire to beat anybody at this or that ; no desire to
accumulate money ; no concern about next year. I
was still very much of a young idiot. All I had in
that way was perhaps a desire to emulate—to tell a
story as ably as Ambrose Bierce and to see and write
as clearly as Stephen Crane.

A further factor took the red light out of their
warnings. Had they shown any marks of misery and
penury, any scars of what they presented as a harrow-
ing struggle, I still would not have accepted their
warnings but I would at least have paid attention.
They showed nothing of the kind. Though they all
said they were poor, and were racked by the struggle of
depending on their work, they all looked very easy and
contented, and were certainly more cheerful and
entertaining and fully alive than any of the well-to-do
and secure whom I had encountered. When they spoke
of the stress and anxiety of the literary life, and its
dolours, and advised me to read Gissing's *New Grub
Street* (which I did), I could only surmise that they had
had no opportunity of comparing the literary life with
life in a commercial office in Fenchurch Street. So I
ignored their advice and followed their example.

When, many years later, I was in my turn asked to
advise young beginners, I gave just the opposite advice.
I told them to throw up everything, to plunge in and
take their chance. I told them not to embrace a dull
certainty and lose a shining risk, not to become a piece
of office furniture in what is called a job for life but is
most often a job for death. Life is risk. Life is a
continual breaking away, snapping of chains, moving
forward to that goal which always recedes. Better be

sorry, I told them, than be everlastingly and odiously safe.

.   .   .   .   .

The literary world, at the time I began writing in the opening years of this century, was, like life generally at that time, much more variegated, less set than it is to-day.   The profession was not as overcrowded as it now is, when half the population seem to be authors, and the young beginner had many more openings for his work.   He had a larger number of periodicals among which to adventure with his occasional writing, and though publishers were not so many then as now, they were all alert for the new writer with a note of his own.   Also, the technical standards of the time were not so high.   This may be seen by looking over the leading " popular " authors.   To modern judgment they make a not very distinguished list, and only a few of them are read, or are readable, to-day.   Those who are still read are mainly the story-tellers.   The most quickly forgotten were those who presented slices of contemporary life, not with too close fidelity, or " problems " which the years have solved.

First in popular esteem were the neck-and-neck rivals, Hall Caine and " Marie Corelli " (originally Minnie Mackay).   Next to them came Rider Haggard, Anthony Hope, Conan Doyle, " Seton Merriman," Stanley Weyman, Maurice Hewlett, Gilbert Parker, " John Oxenham," E. F. Benson, Marion Crawford, Agnes and Egerton Castle, Israel Zangwill, S. R. Crockett, Jerome K. Jerome, Barry Pain, Pett Ridge, W. W. Jacobs, Mrs. Humphry Ward, Beatrice Harraden, Ellen Thorneycroft Fowler, " Lucas Malet," Maria Albanesi, " John Oliver Hobbes," Mary Cholmondeley and Elinor Glyn.   Above the lot of them towered Kipling.   Henry James, George Moore and Yeats were the private property of the elect ; Hardy, Meredith and Swinburne received reverence in Olympian semi-retirement ;   and the advance-guard were talking of certain of the newer men who were not then widely known—John Galsworthy, G. K. Chesterton, Arnold Bennett, Walter de la Mare, Joseph Conrad, Hilaire Belloc, W. H. Hudson, Somerset Maugham. Publishers were making a good deal of splash with translations of Tolstoy, Gorki and the Hungarian, Maurus Jokai, and they were becoming a fashion.

Conditions in the theatre were somewhat similar. The leading dramatists were Pinero, H. A. Jones, H. H. Davies, Robert Marshall, Alfred Sutro, Haddon Chambers, R. C. Carton and Sydney Grundy. Most of them were " drawing-room " dramatists with so narrow an experience of English life that they seemed to think that all English homes were mansions with morning-rooms, conservatories, butlers and footmen, and that no English people were worth presenting in drama except those recognised by Debrett. Their characters were stock figures, and the scenery and props for one of their plays would have served for all the others. None of them is played to-day or, I fancy, even read. Ibsen, Shaw, Maeterlinck, Hauptmann and Sudermann were, like Henry James and George Moore and Meredith, the property of the elect who liked to think that nobody but themselves could understand them.

Every West End theatre at that time had its individual note and its fixed actor-manager, so that audiences knew that at any given theatre they could be sure of seeing a certain actor and actress in a certain kind of play. Irving had left the Lyceum ; but Tree was established at His Majesty's, Cyril Maude at the Haymarket, Arthur Bourchier at the Garrick, George Alexander at the St. James's, Sir Charles Wyndham at the Wyndham, Lewis Waller at the Imperial. The policy of each theatre was set and known. Patrons of His Majesty's knew that whatever they might see there it would not be uproarious farce, and patrons of the Criterion knew that they were safe from any reflection of the grimness of life, while patrons of Drury Lane knew that they would be troubled by no problem, no moral purpose, no exposure of social scandal, no presentation of any kind of life known to any of them.

In journalism, Chesterton, who was then fresh and exciting in a form that later became a formula, was doing a regular Saturday article in the *Daily News*, which had just forsworn all racing and betting news and all drink advertisements ; James Douglas was the literary critic, or rather, literary enthusiast of the *Star*, who every Friday whirled us down his column in a maelstrom of superlatives ; Max Beerbohm was dramatic critic of the *Saturday Review ;* Robertson Nicoll was editing three papers (the *British Weekly*, *British Monthly* and *Bookman*) and was being four people at once as W. R. N., Claudius Clear, O. O., and Man of Kent ; and Arnold Bennett was ordering young men's lives in a series of Savoir-Faire Papers in *T.P's Weekly* under the pseudonym of The Man Who Does.

The young beginner, as I say, had a wide field in the daily, weekly and monthly press. London had ten morning papers : *The Times* at threepence, six others at a penny, and three at a halfpenny. It had nine evening papers : five at a penny, and four at a halfpenny. The now-vanished morning papers were the *Standard, Morning Leader, Daily Chronicle, Morning Post* and *Daily Graphic.* The *Daily Graphic* was the first of the illustrated dailies, and was illustrated at that time mainly with pen-and-ink sketches. The vanished evening papers were the *Globe* (on pink paper), *Westminster Gazette* (on green), *Pall Mall Gazette* and *St. James's Gazette*, all at a penny ; and the *Echo* and the *Sun*, both on pink paper at a halfpenny. The *Echo* was the first of all the halfpenny papers.

The penny papers, especially those of the evening, did not much concern themselves with red-hot news of ordinary daily life. They covered national and international politics, finance and sport, and for the rest they were filled with comment, essays, light sketches and correspondence. Their general note was of an intelligence which no daily journalism of these times approaches. They took for granted in their readers a standard of interest and comprehension which no modern editor would believe in or dare to assume. Their essays and sketches were not written in words of one syllable ; the range of subjects was not confined to the horizon of the clerk and the shop-assistant ; and in literary quality they ranked a good deal higher than most of the books of that time. A prominent feature was the correspondence ; so prominent that it produced a phenomenon in the form of established letter-writers to the press. Foremost among these was Algernon Ashton, who had so many letters printed in the daily and weekly press on such a variety of topics beside his favourite topic of the tombs of the famous, that he was able to publish a volume of selections from them. Other practitioners in the art of " writing to the papers " were J. Landfear Lucas and the Rev. J. M. Bacon-Phillips. It is an art that has now fallen out of cultivation.

The leading articles of the penny papers had a weight and authority nowhere carried to-day, but the evening papers maintained a note of lightness, even levity. The halfpenny papers particularly took their daily task-work with a levity that has no place in a mech-anised million-circulation Fleet Street. The *Star* was always noted for its happy headlines and contents bills (" French President Welcomed at Dover. Tous les Winners et S.P."). And the *Sun*, then owned by Horatio Bottomley, invented a new catch-halfpenny dodge by getting well-known people ostensibly to edit the paper for one day and spread their personalities all over the special articles, the news, and the headlines. On one day it would appear under the editorship of Dr. Parker, of the City Temple ; another day it would be edited by Dan Leno, with an easily foreseen effect ; another day some popular sporting figure would have control, and the staff would treat the contents of each page in terms of his known character and opinions.

L

A remarkable feature of the journalism of those opening years of the century was the mass of penny weeklies of the " bits " kind appealing to the simple and semi-literate. They derived from the success of the pioneer paper in that kind—George Newnes' *Tit-Bits*, which began in the 'eighties. Two young men had written for that paper in its first years and, noting its wide appeal, they went off and started similar papers of their own. Alfred Harmsworth started *Answers*, and Arthur Pearson started *Pearson's Weekly*. Similar things were *Cassell's Saturday Journal*, the *Penny Magazine*, *Penny Pictorial*, *Spare Moments*, *Short Stories*, the *Easy Chair*, *Men and Women*, *Science Siftings*, the *Golden Penny*, the *Coloured Pictorial*, *Sketchy Bits*, *Illustrated Bits*, *Modern Society*, and *Household Words*—revived for a short time by Hall Caine. There were also a number of similar papers named by initials. T. P. O'Connor began it with *M.A.P.* (Mainly About People) and followed it with *P.T.O.* Others were *B.P.*, *V.C.*, and *T.A.T.*, the last standing for Tales and Talk. On a slightly higher level were *T.P.'s Weekly*, the *Free Lance*, the *Candid Friend*, *Black and White*, *Penny Illustrated Paper*, *To-Day* and the *Pelican*. Of all these, only two survive ; the pioneer and its first follower—*Tit-Bits* and *Answers*.

At the same time there was a wide range of sixpenny fiction monthlies, only one of which is with us to-day, and again it is a George Newnes pioneer : in an altered form the *Strand Magazine* still appears. The now-vanished others were the *English Illustrated*, the *Idler*, the *Windsor*, the *London*, *Pearson's*, the *Royal*, the *Novel*, the *Pall Mall*, the *Smart Set*, *Cassell's Magazine*, the *Grand*, the *Lady's Realm*, the *Girls' Realm*. Almost all these monthlies, as well as the weeklies and dailies, then ran serials, so that while the popular novelist of that time did not have the benefit of film-rights he could always pick up £1,000 to £1,500 for serialisation, and at the purchasing values of that time those sums were worth almost as much as to-day's film-right thousands. In serious journalism there were a number of weeklies and monthlies for which modern impatience has no more use than it has for the long leisurely columns of the evening papers of the past. Among them were the *Athenæum, Academy, Outlook, Week's Survey, Pilot, Independent Review, Vanity Fair, Albany Review, World, Nation, Review of Reviews* and *Monthly Review.*

The public which George Newnes found waiting to greet his *Tit-Bits* was a public whose elementary education had given it a phenomenal appetite for information. It fairly guzzled information. It had no special use for this information ; it never sought full information on one given subject ; it wanted snacks of detached information on anything and everything, and it took them down without any attempt to digest them or to relate them to real knowledge. It had the child-mind. It wanted to know because it wanted to know. It was most interested in learning that certain things were not generally known ; as that the number of hairs in a cat's fur was greater (or less) than the number of miles between the earth and the sun ; or that the number of matches used in Birmingham in one day would, if put end to end, reach to—well, quite a long way. A similar phenomenal appetite for promiscuous information is to be observed to-day in the number and the nature of the questions submitted to that radio troupe, the Brains Trust.

Alfred Harmsworth, when he followed the lead of George Newnes, had perceived that it was information rather than entertainment that was sought, and his penny weekly was first named *Answers to Correspondents* and consisted almost wholly of answers to Information Wanted. It set out to fill the vacant mind with pages of facts, and it was instantly successful and clearly met a real if inexplicable need. At that time it was considered a novelty, but it was no novelty. There had been a much earlier forerunner ; not the *Tit-Bits* of the 'eighties, but a journal dating as far back as the late seventeenth century. This was the *Athenian Mercury*, started in 1691 on a similar plan—that of filling its pages with answers to the questions of real or mythical correspondents on all sorts of topics. It even antici-pated the Throb Sisters of modern Fleet Street by running a column in which it gave advice on the heart problems of the love-sick or those seeking matrimony, and on the dilemmas of disgruntled husbands and wives. It ran sections on Love and Marriage, on Marvels and Wonders (forerunner of Things Not Generally Known), on Religious Problems and on Miscellaneous Enquiries ; and vacant minds seem to have been proportionately as many then as now, since it had a life of six years.

The disappearance of the " bits " papers does not mean that there has been a rise in popular taste and intelligence. It means, paradoxically, the reverse—a decline from the ability to read letterpress to an ability to do no more than look at still or moving photographs. Where it could once concentrate on a column of simple words it is now able only to take its information, like very young children, through pictures. And even then the pictures have to be explained. Our popular papers will print a picture of two girls bathing from a seaside beach. The picture is quite clearly a picture of two girls bathing from a seaside beach. But the sub-editor has such a contemptuous understanding of his public that he knows it won't do to let it go like that. The public must be told what it is. So he puts a caption to it : The Fine Week-End Took Crowds to the Coast ; Here Are Two Girls Enjoying a Morning Dip.

Alfred Harmsworth and Arthur Pearson, for some time after they launched out for themselves, seem to have played a game of keeping up with each other. Anything that one did was matched by his competitor. Harmsworth started *Answers* in 1888 ; Pearson started *Pearson's Weekly* in 1890. Harmsworth came out with

Home Chat ; Pearson responded with *Home Notes.*
Pearson in 1895 started *Pearson's Magazine ;* Harmsworth in 1898 got level with *Harmsworth's Magazine.*
Harmsworth in 1896 launched the *Daily Mail ;* Pearson
followed in 1900 with the *Daily Express.* Pearson was
a publisher of books as well as weeklies and monthlies,
so Harmsworth launched out as a publisher of books,
but only long enough to learn that book-publishing was
not his province. Pearson in 1907 made an attempt
to buy *The Times,* and failed ; Harmsworth, some time
later, made the attempt and succeeded. And for each
of them the end of his astonishing and breathless career
came in tragic shape.

.   .   .   .   .

My first literary efforts, made in my early teens,
succeeded only with the common penny weeklies of
the kind I have named. Not until I was twenty did
I attain the pages of the monthlies and the sixpenny
weeklies. My first story, accepted, as I said earlier,
when I was sixteen, appeared in one of the " bits "
papers called *Spare Moments,* which every week offered
one guinea for the best short story sent in. The copy
basket must have been empty the week they gave my
story the prize, but there it was, a full-page, with my
name and address above it, and the morning following
publication brought me a cheque for twenty-one
shillings. Twenty-one shillings may seem pitiful payment for a short story, even a dud story, but when I
report what I was able to buy with it forty-two years
ago nobody can say I was underpaid. With that
twenty-one shillings I had a Soho dinner, a half-bottle
of claret, a West End theatre (pit), three volumes of
the World's Classics, two Canterbury Poets, a box of
the first Turkish cigarettes I smoked (Muratti's Neb-
Ka, in a handsome flat tin), a shirt, two collars and a
tie.
    That first little acceptance looked like an omen of an
easy path, but it wasn't. It was followed by a long

series of rejections. But by the time I was nineteen I was being accepted by another " bits " paper with a leaning to literary topics, called the *Easy Chair*, and had got into the evening paper, the *Echo*, through its front-page " occasional " column, and into that survivor of nineteenth-century saloon-bar humour, *Ally Sloper*. A mixed trio. I had most success with *Ally Sloper*. At that time all sorts of authors and artists who later came to better things were appearing in that paper ; one of them an author who has since become so famous in two continents, and so prosperous with work of a totally different kind, that he would no doubt be annoyed if I publicly recalled his *Ally Sloper* connection. But with all its raffish note it was a pleasant paper to work for ; more pleasant than some of its dignified contemporaries, since it maintained an admirable custom of paying its contributors on the doormat. You could take your manuscript to the office, and somebody would go off with it to an inner office, and you would sit for some minutes in a silence quite incongruous with the paper's front-page. Then the silence would be broken. The cashier of the paper was, I imagine, slightly deaf, because when the silence was broken it was broken by a voice fortissimo bawling, apparently to the cashier, the welcome words, " Give Mr. Burke twenty-five shillings."

In the latter years of that ridiculous paper there was often public discussion as to the true originator of the figure of Ally Sloper. The front page at that time was drawn each week by an artist named W. F. Thomas. But he was not the originator of the figure. Nor was his predecessor, an artist named Baxter. Nor was the first editor of the paper, Charles H. Ross. The figure of Ally Sloper, which no doubt owed something to Micawber, was first created in 1873 before the paper existed. His doings and those of his friend Ikey Mo were first exhibited in the pages of the comic weekly, *Judy*, and his creator was no man. His creator was a woman artist, Marie Duval. Through 1873-4 he had a page to himself in that paper, whose editor was Charles H. Ross, and in 1874 a collection of those pages was issued as a paper-covered volume, *Episodes in the Career of Ally Sloper. 750 Pictures by Marie Duval. One Shilling*. Those pictures so caught the public fancy that Ross thought it worth while to give the figure a paper of its own, and so came *Ally Sloper's Half Holiday*. It lived till about 1909.

The Fleet Street in which I did my early literary adventuring retained features that had stood there through many a lifetime. Among those features were Anderton's Hotel, the Press Café, the Green Dragon, Chilton's sausage-shop, and the Salisbury Hotel in Salisbury Square. All are now gone; only the Cheshire Cheese, the Rainbow, and Groom's Chop House survive all changes and all rebuilding schemes. Features of the Strand of the early 1900's that are now gone were the Golden Cross Hotel, the Lowther Arcade, the Exeter Hall, the Gaiety Hotel, Terry's Theatre, Strand Theatre, Tivoli music-hall, Gow's Chop House and Burgess's Fish Sauce Shop. While Fleet Street, despite physical changes, remains the street of journalism, the Strand has suffered changes not only physical but of spirit. At that time it was the centre of the theatre world. It had seven theatres and a music-hall, and its bars and restaurants were the haunts of actors who announced their calling by their astrakhan-collared coats, their brindled hair, and other accessories by which they sought to pass for second cousins of The Old Man. It had then a definite character, and a life as full and robust as the grocer's Christmas Port. It was the High Street not only of the theatre but of London itself. To-day, the centre of the theatre is the Shaftesbury Avenue region, and the Strand is a nondescript highway of assorted shops in which no business takes precedence.

London at about that time was at the point of changing gears and sliding into a new age of accelerated tempo. The motor-bus had appeared, though it had

not then displaced the horse-bus; they ran side by
side, and often the horse-bus out-sped the experimental
motor-bus. Nor did the first taxis at once displace
the hansom; they, too, ran side by side. The electric
brougham had a brief vogue, and private cars, the
cheapest of which was then about £600, ran alongside
the horse-carriages of the conservative. Old and new
jostled each other for place; not until 1911 did the
last horse-bus leave the streets, and an occasional
hansom could be seen as late as the 1920's.

In entertainment, too, old and new went side by
side. The cinema had arrived, but in a hole-and-
corner way; films were shown in parish-halls and
empty shops, admission twopence and threepence.
They showed then no sign of growing into a million-
dollar industry, ruining the music-hall and damaging
the theatre with shows given in Byzantine and Renaissance palaces. The music-hall and the theatre perceived no threat in the new thing; they regarded it
only as a *maître d'hôtel* might regard a coffee-stall.

Through this period of acceleration London remained
for those with even a modest income a comfortable
city in which one could live at ease. We had then a
personal liberty beyond anything known to the present
State-controlled generation. We could travel from
England to any part of Europe (except Russia) without
passport or landing-ticket or *permis-de-séjour* or *laisser-
passer*, and without giving an outline of our lives at
our hotels. We could buy what we wanted at almost
any hour; in central London all sorts of shops were
open till eight or nine o'clock, and in the suburbs until
eleven, which on Saturdays became midnight. We
could run our shops or our businesses in our own way
without spending hours in filling up sheaves of forms
or being hampered by strings of State inspectors. We
could get a drink at any hour between six in the morning and half-past twelve at night; on Sundays, if we
travelled more than three miles from our home, we
could get a drink at any time of morning, afternoon or

evening up to eleven o'clock. We could, in short, go freely about our affairs without innocently breaking every hour of the day some of the hundred-and-one Whitehall regulations. ,

Income Tax was a shilling in the pound. The well-known brands of cigarettes were sixpence for twenty ; Egyptian were sixpence for ten. A bottle of Bass or Guinness was threepence. A small whisky of one of the famous brands was threepence. A bottle of one of those whiskies was 3s. 6d. You and a friend could go to one of the smartest and most expensive London restaurants and dine à la carte on caviare, soup, sole, lamb, woodcock, asparagus, ice, champagne, coffee and liqueur, and the total bill for the two would be about two guineas. You could go to other smart hotel-restaurants and take their table d'hôte of hors d'œuvres, soup, salmon, quail, saddle of mutton, chicken and salad, strawberries and coffee and petits fours for 5s. 6d. And there were scores of places serving a satisfactory dinner for 3s. 6d. Oysters in West End oyster-bars were 3s. a dozen ; in the suburbs 1s. and even 6d. Your wine-merchant could supply you with a Château-bottled Bordeaux at 48s. a dozen, and everyday beverage wines—Margaux, St. Emilion, St. Julien— at 18s. a dozen. Moselle—a Zeltinger or Braunberger —was 28s. a dozen ; even a Berncasteler Doktor, lilac seal, was only 60s. a dozen. At 30s. a dozen you could also get a drinkable Burgundy—a Volnay or Pommard. A good port could be had at 48s. a dozen and sherry at 3s. a bottle.

In that London I was launched as an author, making a single-handed set at editors. I had no help in this. None of the three or four authors I knew, who had warned me against dependence on literary work, gave me introductions. I was alone, with nobody to open a door or say a word for me, and it may encourage some beginner of to-day to learn that though I could only send in my manuscript as an unknown outsider to a nameless Editor, I came gradually to have my work

accepted at the rate of about one in four. I began as
I have continued, with short stories, London sketches,
and articles on literary topics, and by the time I was
nineteen I had had articles taken on London's Derelict
Markets, Last Poems of Famous Poets, London's
Villages, Forgotten Poets, One-Book Authors ; and
facetious sketches taken by *Ally Sloper* on Carol
Singing, Soho table d'hôtes, Hyde Park Orators, and
so on.

Gissing, in his *Henry Ryecroft*, has a passage asking
whether there was at that time anybody in the circumstances in which he had been twenty years before.
" Is there, at this moment, any boy of twenty, fairly
educated, but without means, without help, with
nothing but the glow in his brain and steadfast courage
in his heart, who sits in a London garret and writes for
dear life ? " And he doubts it. Conditions, he thinks,
have by that time (1902) changed and all the young
writers he hears of eat at fashionable restaurants and
inhabit handsome flats and belong to reputable clubs
and keep extensive wardrobes. But he was wrong.
At the time I read that passage (1903) he was still
alive, and I felt like writing to him and telling him that
I knew of at least one young man who at that moment
was in just the state and circumstances that had been
his.

Only unlike him, I was well content. I had escaped
from office drudgery, and I was engaged as I wished
to be, working if not in the literary world at least on
its outskirts—where I have been ever since. It is true
that while for the last forty-two years I have lived for
and by literature I have never at any time in any real
sense been " in " the literary world. I have worked
as a professional and somehow lived as an amateur.
This was not on my part intentional ; it just happened
that way. Nobody ever asked me in.

With my days and nights of writing I continued to
mix a vast and miscellaneous reading. I never
" studied " English literature or engaged in any

academic " course of reading." I read only what I
wanted to read, and never for anything but my own
pleasure, but in that way I covered the greater part of
English literature. By the time I was twenty I had
read the major English writers and many of the minor,
but there were a few gaps, and in my new freedom I
was able to fill them. I filled them with the eight
volumes of Arber's *English Garner*, the three volumes
of Hindley's *Book Collector's Miscellany*, the publica-
tions of the Early English Text Society, the old
chroniclers, the early English itineraries and the
" character " writers. At that time all sorts of oddments of the seventeenth and eighteenth centuries, to
be had to-day only at collector's prices, could be picked
up for a few pence on the barrows of Farringdon Street,
and there I found a number of obscure things not in
Arber or Hindley—memoirs of the unknown, journals,
pamphlets on abuses of the times, satires and moral
disquisitions, the spent powder of dead controversies,
the Letters and Remains of nobodies, travel-diaries of
the unobservant ; the trivia of the book world ; but
all of them written with regard for English. None of
them was scribbled. Bad writing did not begin before
the early nineteenth century.

Through this byway reading, and through my earlier
years of reading for my own pleasure the standard
novels, plays, essays, diaries, letters, biographies, I
acquired unconsciously and by the way a close knowledge of the detail of social history—how people of any
given period were living, what they were talking about,
what idioms they were using, what they were wearing
and eating and drinking, what their homes and their
habits were. When I came years later to write
anecdotal histories of the street-life of London, of
English night-life and English travel, of the English
inn and the English townsman, I had no need to engage
in research. I had it all in my head. Research is
something I have never done and would hate to do.
All I needed for those books I had already taken in,

and with the help of an acute memory what had been a desultory pleasure became pertinent and profitable.

While I was still clinging to my precious freedom of days, a little job of an interesting kind was offered to me, and as it did not interfere with my daytime hours, and as acceptances of my work were spasmodic, I took it. It was a Fleet Street job which demanded only my evenings.

In 1906 a new morning paper in the Liberal interest was presented to the public, and a novel method of advertising it was used. On the day of its first issue Londoners on their way to work found all London's bus-horses caparisoned in white cloths, bearing the legend : *The Tribune. One Penny Daily. All the News that is Fit to Print.* It was on that paper that I took the job of secretary to the Foreign Editor at hours from six to midnight. Its offices, newly built, were in Bouverie Street, and at night their exterior was illuminated by long thin lamps with a then-new kind of illuminant which shed a ghastly green about the street. On the ground floor was an Enquiry Bureau established for the benefit of that large class with an appetite for information, where you could ask any question you could think of. It was called The Tribune Rendezvous, and it provided not only the Enquiry Bureau but a Reading Room, Reference Library, and a Lecture Hall in which lectures on current topics were given by Experts—all free to the public.

Philip Gibbs was the literary editor of the paper, and around it and its brief life he built his novel *The Street of Adventure*. That brief life, if it proved anything, proved that the day was past when readers would appreciate a sober newspaper with a fine literary quality pervading all its columns. Corrupted as they had been by imitations of the snap and zip of American journalism, they found the *Tribune* too solid and slow.

My job in those elaborate offices was the kind of job that appealed to me. It was light and easy, and most of the evening I spent in writing my own stuff. The little work I did do was to answer a few of the Foreign Editor's letters and to take his dictation of the foreign leader. As I could always type at speed— Stanley Unwin once said I was the fastest typist he had ever seen or heard—I was able to save time by taking his dictation straight on to the typewriter, and to use the saved time for myself.

I was engaged in that idly-busy way one evening when a member of the literary staff who had noted both my speed and my idleness asked if I would make a copy of something for him. I said Certainly, and did it. I was then twenty and a free-lance journalist on my own, but I have always looked less than my years, and I then looked about fifteen. So I suppose he was doing what he thought was suitable to the occasion when he offered me half a crown. I assured him that the little job had meant no trouble and waved the half-crown away. Whereupon he went off and in less than a minute came back and presented me with a pocket edition of *Virginibus Puerisque*, which he asked me to accept and which, to save him embarrassment, I just had to accept.

In the summer of 1907 the paper came to sudden death ; so sudden that it was a matter of minutes. I left the office at midnight, and everything was going as usual. But some time after midnight, as I learned later, the proprietor came down to the office and wrote a paragraph which was to be boxed on the front page. I saw it at breakfast next morning. The issue that was going on the machines when I left the office was the last issue of the *Tribune*. And the end of the last enterprise in purely English journalism.

The daily journalism of to-day has shed its old-time sobriety. In our million-circulation newspapers the presentation of the news reflects the spirit of this breathless age. It is reflected too in the many regular features : in the social gossip column, the crazy column, the streamer headline across the whole page, head-

lines of six words without a verb among them, the use
of the front-page for news, the very language or jargon-
phrases in which the news of the popular press is
written and the whole make-up of the paper. All these
features have been introduced so gradually that few
people have noted them. Before the last war, even
in the popular press, all articles on the leader page
began with a single modest title at the top of a single
solid column and finished at the bottom. There were
cross-heads but no article was run in two half-columns
or across four columns. Each page was column after
column, with no white spaces, no flaring capitals, no
long sub-titles to the articles. If you were to show
a school-boy of to-day a newspaper of 1912 he would
pronounce it unreadable.

．　　　．　　　．　　　．　　　．

My chief recreation at that time, next to reading,
was the music-hall, and I spent many an evening, not
at the local Imperial Palace nor at the Alhambra or
Empire, but at the Tivoli, the Oxford and the London
Pavilion. There one could see in one evening, for a
matter of two shillings, eighteen or twenty stars. One
could see Ernest Shand with his grotesque curates;
Chirgwin, the White-Eyed Kaffir, who was as Cockney
as Camberwell; Sam Mayo, the Immobile One; Gus
Elen, with his coster-songs; Marie Lloyd, who was
Marie Lloyd; George Robey, who was George Robey;
Mark Sheridan, with bell-bottomed trousers and French
stove-pipe hat; T. E. Dunville, a sort of Saturday-
night back-street pierrot; Phil Ray, with spluttered
songs made up of abbreviated words; Harry Tate,
with his adventures in Motoring, Golfing or Fishing
presented in dishevelled sketches of everyday life shot
with lucid intervals of lunacy; Ella Retford with her
Lancashire-Irish songs; Wilkie Bard creating a world
of his own in which nothing could be taken for granted;
Dutch Daly with a concertina and a stream of stories;
Harry Lauder, who was Harry Lauder; Cinquevalli,

who turned juggling into poetry ; George Mozart, with shrill, acid sketches of types from any suburban High Street ; Little Tich, who was indescribable ; Vesta Tilley with her young-men characters ; the American R. G. Knowles, with the husky voice and the machine-gun hail of broad anecdote—all these you could see in one bill, in the circle for two shillings, in the pit for a shilling, and in the gallery for sixpence.

From those evenings of grotesquerie I caught again the thrill of contact with real life that I had found in those keen moments of my childhood. It was not the real life of the poets and musicians, but it was more alive than anything in the routine of streets and houses. It held the essence of man's daily war with all the things that are against his realisation of dignity and godship ; his circumstances, his clothes, his furniture, his appetites, his friends, all were shown as conspiring against him, tripping and impeding every approach to his noble estate just below the angels. In all that apparent idiocy, behind all those macabre masks, was the passion of life itself, felt and lived. In the angles and arabesques of that contorted world I found more truth than in the theatre or the street. Under the lunatic jargon of the songs and the monstrous costumes was a logic not of intellect but of poetry, drawn from the midnight deeps of the subconscious. When the music-hall died I lost a source of delight. Nothing of the kind is to be had to-day. Our deliberately " crazy " comedians and " crazy " shows, imitations of American vaudeville, have nothing of the true, native, spon-taneous lunacy. You cannot reduce logic to the irrational or carry lunacy to the height of sense by deliberation ; it must spring, as it did with those older men, from life and habit.

Another recreation of mine at that time was the indulgence of that passion of which I have spoken for seeing England. Outside London and with the excep-tion of Hertfordshire, I knew nothing of my country, and I wanted to know all about it and to go all over it, and at last in a modest way I was able to do it. Every now and then an accepted article or short story helped me to make little excursions to towns that had long been promising names to me and nothing more. Most of the railways then had a custom of running long-distance day-trips at incredibly cheap fares to all places of historic or general interest on their lines, and incredibly cheap fares were just about what I was able, for the first time, to afford. I went on scores of those day-trips. The most delightful were those of the Great Western, and Paddington became for me a portal to all manner of beauty and stimulus. It opened on days up the river at Taplow and Maidenhead, Henley, Sonning, and along the serene and pastoral reaches linking Pangbourne, Goring and Wallingford and their forget-me-not and cowslip meadows and their rose-garden inns.

I made a particular point, in my youthful naïveté, of going on literary pilgrimages—to Stoke Poges (Gray), to Beaconsfield (Waller), to Horton and Chalfont (Milton), to Laleham (Matthew Arnold), to Marlow (Shelley), to Chertsey (Cowley), to Halliford (Peacock). Middlesex and Buckinghamshire were my Poets' Country, and though they are now becoming urban the landscapes in the few still rural corners and along the river are poets' landscapes. They have the morning light and accent of English lyrics, they speak of youth, where moors and mountains speak of age, and among them one can feel how the songs of those poets grew from just that kind of landscape.

Most satisfying were the longer excursions—to Bath 3s. return ; to Oxford 3s. return ; and to Stratford, Warwick, Banbury, Exeter, Hereford, and even Tintern Abbey—all for 4s. return. I recall shining summer mornings at Paddington, and the excitement of taking train to places whose names had a nimbus of bright association, and of wondering whether the place would fulfil its legend. All around me were people also of my mood—not the preoccupied travellers of the business stations or the hot and ungainly crowds of those stations serving the south-east " seaside resorts," but an easy crowd, going coolly up the river or to the spas or to western cathedral towns. And then there was the gliding out of the dim, sun-fretted station into the full sunlight, and through the western suburbs, and between banks of wild flowers, and so along the Thames, and then a stop at some, to me unknown, station where the refreshment wagon came along and boys with trays cried Banbury Cakes or Leamington Cakes. And after the experience of the town I was visiting, which was always satisfying since I was prepared to be satisfied, there was the equally delightful long journey home through the shining evening fields, and then through the twilight with cottage lamps sparking the horizon, and then the plush darkness and then the run into Paddington which was at that hour a little cathedral holding a sort of evensong of holiday.

The delight I experienced on those little trips in my own country may afford amusement to those who were free at any age to move about Europe, but, as I said earlier, I had been debarred by want of pence from any movement for many years, and the mere train-travelling, which to other people was a nuisance, was to me a new pleasure. I grew in time to tire of it but never to tire of seeing new towns either in England or Europe. Those tentative day-trips from Paddington and from the other London stations to all sorts of odd places, some that filled me with rapture and some that brought only interesting experience, were the beginning of what were to be month-long wanderings across England by rail, car and on foot. At that time they had, like my miscellaneous reading, no purpose save personal pleasure, but through them I acquired a knowledge of English towns and villages, highways and green roads and old inns, that was later turned to a purpose in certain of my books.

The casual journalism by which I was supporting

M

myself took many forms : articles, short stories, sketches, verses, and a new kind of interview known as the " signed article." For this you interviewed your well-known man, got his views on a particular subject, wrote an article expressing his views in the first person, and sent it to him for signature. The article appeared as by the well-known man, and the fee was yours. There were then many openings for verse. The *Westminster Gazette* and *Pall Mall Gazette* used verse every day, and verses of mine appeared frequently in both papers and in the *Nation*, the *Pall Mall Magazine*, the *Sphere,* the *Graphic*, the *New Age*, *Chambers's Journal*, *Daily Chronicle*, and a monthly devoted entirely to verse, called the *Thrush*. Stories and sketches were being taken by the popular magazines, and occasional articles by the weekly papers. I remember the *Idler* taking four short stories of mine, and sending me a cheque for £5 for the four, with which I was not dissatisfied ; so you can guess what sort of income I was making.

I was quite unknown and had, as I say, no introductions to editors, and I was constantly surprised by the kindness of editors, and the trouble they took in showing me where and why my work was wrong, and how it might be made right, and in generally encouraging me. As editors are seldom known beyond their generation, and as they are mostly men of an urbane, even gracious temperament, and of a goodwill rarely met in other professions, I would like here to celebrate Wilfred Whitten of *T.P.'s Weekly*, J. P. Collins, literary editor of the *Pall Mall Gazette* and assistant-editor of the *Pall Mall Magazine* ; A. W. Evans, assistant-editor of the *Nation* ; Orage, of the *New Age* ; Percy Everett, editor of *Pearson's Magazine* ; James Milne, literary editor of the *Daily Chronicle* ; J. M. Bulloch, of the *Graphic* ; and D. M. Sutherland, of I forget what paper, who paid me the first literary compliment I ever received in a reference to my " vigorous, picturesque descriptive."

The stories I was writing at that time were of various kinds but all of them had somewhere a common undertone. In Geneva Street, in the High Street of my suburb, in that orchard, in that dream, and in my long wanderings about the lost corners of London I had been in the land of faery, and what I knew when I was there I tried to convey in my stories. Not directly, since most of my stories, past and present, are of the rather grim kind ; but indirectly ; that is, conveying one thing under cover of apparently conveying something quite different.

A puzzle to many an author is that of the genesis and growth of his stories. The oddest thing will start a story, usually something that bears no traceable relation to the story in its completed form. A story of mine concerned solely with Chinese people in the docks district of London began to grow from a little incident between two farmers witnessed in the market-place of Aylesbury. Another, concerning a series of murders, grew from a haberdasher's window making a display of white woollen gloves. From the sight of a hilarious young actor in the Savoy Grill came my novel, *The Sun in Splendour*, which nowhere introduces hilarity or actors. Reading a report of the will of a rich man who left £100,000 for scientific research started a train of thought from which grew my little novel, *The Flower of Life*, which has nothing to do with bequests or scientific research ; it is the life-story of a domestic servant. The sight of the bomb-wrecked Paternoster Row started something that produced my novel, *Victorian Grotesque*, set in a world far from the world of books or bombs ; and a report of the building of new film-studios at Denham, near Uxbridge, led me to writing the story, *Murder at Elstree*, the story of Thurtell's murder of William Weare in 1823. But whether anything of their genesis appears in any of these stories or not, whether they are grim or gracious, they are all fairy-tales.

I still have some odd copies of the illustrated fiction

magazines of my youth, forty years ago, and they afford
interesting glimpses on a world—a literary and a social
world—that is gone. No doubt they would appear as
" old-fashioned " to young people of to-day, as volumes
of *Temple Bar* and the *Argosy* used to appear to me ;
but in their time they were well done. The *Pall Mall
Magazine* of 1904, for example, had as contributors
George Moore, Fielding Hall, Maurice Hewlett, G. S.
Street, Marriott-Watson, William Archer, and William
Sharp and his shadow " Fiona Macleod." For illus-
trations it had D. Y. Cameron, Maurice Grieffenhagen,
Russell Flint, Claude Shepperson, S. H. Sime, Edmund
Sullivan and Norman Wilkinson. The *Windsor*'s chief
contributors were Kipling, Anthony Hope, Eden
Phillpotts, Rider Haggard, H. C. Bailey, Jack London,
H. A. Vachell, Phillips Oppenheim, Quiller-Couch ; and
its chief artists were Fred Pegram, Harry Furniss,
Penrhyn Stanlaws, F. H. Townshend, Cyrus Cuneo.
The *London* (which set out to knock its rivals by
offering a magazine of the same size and number of
pages as theirs at $3\frac{1}{2}d.$, when theirs, published at $6d.$,
sold at $4\frac{1}{2}d.$) had stories by Marie Corelli, Lloyd
Osbourne, Arthur Morrison, Richard le Gallienne, and
illustrations by T. Heath Robinson, H. M. Brock,
Albert Morrow, John H. Bacon, Stanley L. Wood and
Sidney Paget.

Sidney Paget was the original illustrator of the
Sherlock Holmes stories as they appeared in the *Strand*,
and the instant success of those stories fifty years ago
started a literary fashion which is still a fashion.
Conan Doyle in all innocence fathered a progeny as
prolific as the seed of Abraham. He set the editors of
all the other magazines looking for something of a
similar kind, and Sherlock Holmes became the sire of
Arthur Morrison's Martin Hewitt, Christie Murray's
John Pym, Headon Hill's Zambra, Dick Donovan's
Vincent Trill, L. T. Meade's Doctor with his Diary,
Hesketh Pritchard's Flaxman Low, Guy Boothby's
Dr. Nikola, Baroness Orczy's Old Man in the Corner,

Fletcher Robinson's Addington Peace, Harold Begbie's
Andrew Latter, and a group of others, not forgetting
the boys' own Sherlock Holmes, who seems to have
been given the elixir of life—Sexton Blake. Since
those days the line has developed through Dr. Thorn-
dyke and Father Brown to Hanaud, Poirot, Dr.
Priestley, Mr. Fortune, Roger Sheringham, Mrs. Brad-
ley, Anthony Gethryn, Colonel Gore, and half a hundred
collaterals. A social historian of three hundred years
from now might be excused if, judging us by our
magazines and novels, he drew the inference that crime
was the paramount feature of the social life of the first
half of the twentieth century, and the private investi-
gation of it one of the major professions.

The advertisement pages of those old magazines
throw sharp sidelights on the byways of social history.
Judging from the medical advertisements the chief
physical troubles of that time were rupture, alcoholic
excess, anæmia and baldness. Each issue contains
many advertisements of remedies for these troubles.
George R. Sims' hair-restorer Tatcho and Edwards'
Harlene are advertised in almost every number, and
many advertisements offer methods of both How To
Get Thin and How To Get Fat. Sandow offers his
Muscle Developers and other advertisers offer their
Electric Belts for Manly Vigour. One issue has four
advertisements of How To Influence Others by
Hypnotism and Personal Magnetism ; others offer to
tell you How to Get Tall and How to Develop a Bust.
Solid silver watches are offered at 25s., and complete
dinner services, direct from the Five Towns, for one
guinea. Bedroom suites are ten guineas, and Melba's
first records, made for the Gramophone Company, and
just issued, are offered at one guinea each. The most
surprising advertisement perhaps is that of a tooth-
paste with a testimonial from Verdi, whose letter is
said to have been one of the last he wrote just before
his death in 1901.

Many of my kindly editors in advising me echoed each other with the advice—" Why don't you write a novel ? That's the best way towards establishing yourself." But I had no desire to write a novel. The novel form did not attract me. I was drawn almost wholly to the short-story form and to the many bright adventures which it offered in the many ways in which one could carve in ebony or ivory a moment's monument. There is as great a gulf between the novel and the short story as between the epic and the sonnet ; and few men are specialist in both. The novelist and the writer of the short story may again be likened to the actor and the music-hall artist. The actor has two or three hours in which to make his effect, and is supported by others ; the music-hall artist is alone, and he has only a matter of minutes in which to make his effect, and so must capture his audience in the first few seconds and keep them with the concentration of his whole being. So the novelist has a spacious field in which he may move at leisure, and a group of characters to help him maintain the burden of his theme, while the short-story writer has only about five thousand words in which to move, and must therefore catch his reader in his first sentences.

Trollope once complained of being in a dilemma. He had to write a short story for a Christmas Number, and he marked the difference between having to write a short story and having a short story to write. It is the fault of the young beginner in the short story that he is too often in Trollope's dilemma. He sits down to write a short story before he is sure that he has a story to write. He catches at the first shred of an idea that comes along and dashes gaily into writing it, instead of living with it for a week or two, looking all round it, and satisfying himself that it is a story, that it is original, and that his method of presentation is the right method.

Generally he has no very clear sense of what a short story *is*. It is a common mistake of the beginner to assume that a dramatic event of real life will translate itself into an equally dramatic short story, or that what would be an effective subsidiary episode in a novel will make an effective short story. A short story must be a single and self-contained work, at one or two removes from actual life and its clustering contingencies, with nothing to be assumed before it begins and nothing save a mental reverberation after its end. It must have body as well as frame. Every paragraph must carry it forward. Everything in it must be an integral part of its theme and help to lead it to its inevitable end. It must not merely stop ; it must satisfyingly end.

The short story of to-day is of two kinds ; what is called the Magazine Story, and the newer kind which derives from Europe and is cultivated by the more exclusive reviews. The latter is not really a short story. It has no true beginning and only a nebulous conclusion. It is not concerned with telling a tale, but rather with presenting a situation, with illumination of commonplace incident, with revelation of the secret corners of mind or character, or distillation of the essence of some transitory mood. It is of its time— frigid in attitude and metallic in tone. It is something apart, and should have a term to itself.

The short story of tradition, the tradition maintained by the magazines, is always a story. It has a beginning, a crux and a climax. By advanced readers and writers it is scorned, yet people both simple and subtle still ask for a story. So the short story truly named must first of all be a story. It must hold the attention of the reader so surely that he will go on reading even when the sun is shining and the tennis court is waiting. Its people must be alive ; in the mere flash of time covered by the short story they must come so alive that the reader will know them instantly and remember them. Their problem or predicament must be pre- sented so as to win his concern ; the writer must have the mariner's glittering eye and with it hold his reader

from all other allurements.   If he cannot do that he is
not a born story-teller.

We all know a real short story when we meet it, and
each of us can supply examples from his own reading.
A few of my own favourites, stories which begin at the
beginning and move to an inevitable end, are *The
Beckoning Fair One* (Oliver Onions), *The Monkey's
Paw* (W. W. Jacobs), *The Tiger Skin* (Violet Hunt),
Alias Jimmy Valentine (O. Henry) *The Broken Shutter*
(Ambrose Bierce), *The Doll's Ghost* (Marion Crawford),
The Lady or the Tiger (Frank Stockton), *Mrs. Rivers'
Journal* (Perceval Landon), *What Was It?* (Fitz-James
O'Brien) *Rain of Dollars* (Quiller-Couch), *The Silver
Mask* (Hugh Walpole), *The Man Who Liked Dickens*
(Evelyn Waugh).

Another common mistake of the beginner, even when
he has a story, is that he follows outmoded forms.   One
finds him using the clumsy machinery of presenting
his story as narrated by a man in a club or a hotel
lounge.   Once in a way a story comes for which that
method is apt ; is, indeed, a necessary part of its
atmosphere ; but generally there is no good cause why
the story should be told through a narrator.   The
verisimilitude is not heightened, nor does it gain in
atmosphere or dramatic quality.   Indeed, this attempt
to give an air of reality almost always succeeds in
destroying it, where a straight presentation by the
author would assure it.

Another and more dangerous mistake is that of
using the wrong tone and accent.   I lately read four
short stories by one young author.   The four stories
were markedly different in theme and characters and
setting, and for all four stories he had used the same
pedestrian tone.   The same descriptive epithets appeared in all four, and the ring of the dialogue of one
story was the same as that of the other three.   But
every story is a new story, and if it is to achieve its
effect it must carry the peculiar accent and rhythm fit
to its telling.   One kind of story demands the casual,

colloquial tone; another demands the quiet adagio tone; another the tone of urgency, and yet another the murmur of reverie. By constant practice the true story-teller is eventually guided by instinct to the right tone for each particular story.

As we know a short story when we meet it, so we know the thing that isn't. An account of two lovers having a misunderstanding and, after much pain, clearing it up, is not a short story unless the author can make that lovers' quarrel, in its atmosphere and situation, unlike any other lovers' quarrel and yet, in its impact, universal. Again, a story of a woman leaving her husband for another man, and then finding that the despised husband is the one man who pays her the high compliment of really needing her, has been told many times. It was a short story once, and only once. But Evelyn Waugh's story of *The Man Who Liked Dickens* had never been told until he told it. That is why it sticks in the mind.

And that in itself is a test of the short story—is it with you five years after reading it? If the young beginner would think of that when devising and writing his story, he would select his idea with greater care, and would write it with such urgency to impress it upon his reader that it would become a real story and would be remembered. There is an anecdote pertinent to this of the Victorian preacher, Spurgeon. A young candidate for ordination asked Spurgeon if he would hear privately his first attempt at a sermon. Spurgeon heard him, and when it was done he said, " Yes. Excellently done. A very beautiful discourse. But quite useless. What you're doing in that sermon, my boy, is *expressing yourself*. Your task as a preacher is to *impress* your *congregation*. Not to get something out of yourself but to get something into them." That applies to all the arts, and particularly to the short story, which, because it is short, must impress the reader in the first few moments or for ever lose him. The first thing is to have a story. Then to tell it with so glittering an eye that the reader is held against his will and feels it as oneself felt it.

I don't know that I have ever myself accomplished that. I know I have made all the mistakes I have named here, and I know, after forty years of story-telling, that I have fallen short of my own target of success. In those early 1900's my favourite among the illustrated magazines, and the standard against which I judged all magazines, was *Harper's*. *Harper's*, with its fine illustrations and its articles and stories from Mark Twain, W. D. Howells, Edith Wharton, Henry James, Mary Wilkins, Margaret Deland, Arthur Symons. I used then to think that if and when I had a story in *Harper's* I would be able to feel that I was really and truly an author, a full member of the literary world. That was in 1904 or 1905. It is now 1945, and I have never yet had a story in *Harper's*. It may be because I have never offered it a story, but there it is ; I am not yet to my own satisfaction a full and adult author.

CHAPTER X

OCCASIONS AND ENCOUNTERS

"I'VE read those five things of yours, my boy. Four of 'em don't amount to much. Just competent modern journalism. But the other one—Monkeys' Parade—that's good, because it's you—individual. The others might have been written by anybody. But that one could only have been written by the man who did write it. And that's the only kind of work that matters. Go on with things like that. Be yourself. And with plenty of practice you ought to succeed."

"But I thought one ought not to be oneself. I

thought one ought to suppress oneself and be detached.
I hesitated about sending you that one. It isn't like
anything I've ever seen in any paper."

" That's its value."

" I thought it was rather raw. No shape to it.
Slapdash."

" Yes, and it's just right. Catches just the right
note. It's alive. And vitality in a work is a darned
sight more important than form and impersonal polish.
You set down there what you really saw and what
you really felt about it. In the others you've set
down what you *thought* you *ought* to see. Forget all
that Flaubertism and go on being yourself."

That advice came from a man whose acquaintance
I made in those early days of free-lancing—the London
novelist, Edwin Pugh. He is now forgotten and even
then was rather in the shade. He had belonged to
the 'nineties when, before he was twenty-one, his first
book, *A Street in Suburbia*, had been published on the
recommendation of Sarah Grand of *The Heavenly
Twins*. On the strength of that he became one of the
W. E. Henley group of the *New Review* and a regular
contributor to Jerome's *Idler* and *To-Day* and many
other papers.

He was a good friend, a good critic, and a talker
with a dry, effervescent wit. He was short and stocky
in build, with a high colour, and hair, before it went
white, of jet-black—altogether Welsh. Except at
occasional periods, when an inherited disability possessed him, he had a winning genial charm of manner
and an expression bubbling with fun. His most
notable feature was his eyes. I have never seen in
any other person such large lustrous brown eyes.
They were such eyes as one sees in horses, but lit with
the fire of the human mind ; deep but alert ; wide
open with interest at the world's spectacle, like a
child regarding his Christmas stocking. But in his
" possessed " periods he was utterly changed. His
eyes lost their light ; his effervescent wit shot un-

accountably into volcanoes of temper ; and his genial current became a flood of black fury.

His work never reached the large public. When he was writing, something seemed to come between him and the paper. Few men are like their work, but in Pugh's case the difference was wide indeed. It was odd that one so warm of temperament, so humorous in talk, so alive to fun (his father had been chief comedian of the Moore and Burgess Minstrels), so aware of the pathos of our little life, should have produced novels so chill and bony and joyless. I believe he approached each book with the intention of filling it with the warmth and pulse of life, but something went wrong between conception and execution. Each novel was the product of keen and deep observation. There was mind in them but not much heart ; emotion but little affection. One explanation of this may be that despite his Celtic origin, he could make no response to music or poetry except in their simplest forms —a seaside band or a nursery rhyme. He saw all things and people with the mind. He had understanding but could give little love. Where he was sympathetic it was by reason not instinct. A devout worshipper of Dickens, he wrote his own novels in the dry, cold light of the French novelists but failed to give them the French vitalising stab and gleam of life. One might adapt to them the excellent bit of music-criticism of the old American humorist, Bill Nye : " Wagner's music is better than it sounds." Pugh's novels were better than they ever appeared to be, and perhaps at some later date the mental sincerity with which they were charged may draw readers to re-discover his best things—*Tony Drum*, *The Eyes of a Child*, *The Great Unborn* and *Punch and Judy*.

He was conscious of failure but quite unbothered about it. His early life had endowed him with a certain bitterness but not his literary life. He was wholly free of any grudging recognition of the success of those whose work was far inferior to his own. His general attitude was " Good luck to 'em." Certain writers of his time he disliked, as men, but he never allowed that feeling to colour his judgment of their work, and I have heard him use the highest terms of praise about the books of men whom personally he detested. With equal honesty he would dismiss inferior work by men with whom he was in sympathy.

His talk, which was a sort of thinking aloud, was salted, as his novels never were, by interjected remarks or murmured asides which, unless you were sitting near him, often went unperceived. They were given an extra tang by the strong London accent in which they were spoken. Thus, of Barry Pain : " Yes, when Barry Pain came down from Cambridge it was said that he might do anything. He did." Of a certain thrusting writer who was always getting into the literary paragraphs : " He's a leading member, they say, of the Bachelors' Club. Shouldn't wonder if his father is too." Of a dead friend : " The operation, as usual, was entirely successful, and the funeral was at Golders Green."

I have just turned up a sheaf of his letters, and they remind me of another characteristic of his, in sharp contrast to his muddled and shiftless way of life—his extraordinarily neat, microscopic but perfectly legible handwriting. On a quarto page he could pack a thousand words, and they were as clear as type. It was the smallest hand I have seen ; smaller even than George Gissing's ; and I have often wondered how a graphologist would have reconciled it with the writer as I knew him.

He was, as I say, of the 'nineties, and many an evening he entertained me with reminiscences of that agitated decade. I have never understood why the 'nineties should have become known as the Beardsley Period when they were so obviously the period of a very different man. The 'nineties were, in a national way, never attained by the Vigo Street group, the

Kipling Period. Still, as the word 'nineties always connotes the Bodley Head and the *Yellow Book* and the *Savoy*, it must stand in that sense. Some of those Vigo Street men Pugh had known, but mostly he had known those who were just as much of the spirit of the 'nineties—the Heinemann group : Sarah Grand, Stephen Crane, Israel Zangwill, W. E. Henley, Conrad, as well as Gissing, Jerome, Frank Harris, Jacobs, Conan Doyle.

He had a stream of anecdote turning on Sunday evenings at Henley's house at Muswell Hill which was then a regular rendezvous for " Henley's Young Men "; of week-ends with Stephen Crane at Brede Place, near Rye, and the incongruous and dishevelled house-parties he gathered there ; of days with H. G. Wells, first at Worcester Park, and later at Sandgate ; of meetings with Ernest Dowson and Lionel Johnson at the Radnor, a public-house that then stood at the Holborn corner of Chancery Lane. Stories of Harold Frederic instructing Henry James how to do it : of Henley roaring and banging and flourishing his crutch at those who differed from him on the merits and faults of writers past and present ; of Frank Harris booming preposterous lies about the Wild West, and entertaining contributors to his papers with elaborate luncheons, which was his form of payment ; of George Gissing's unexpected skill at ball-games and his keen sense of fun ; of A. E. W. Mason as producer of amateur theatricals at Brede Place ; of Conrad mystifying the landlords of country inns with orders for glasses of " bee-tairs." And a hundred other stories of people of that period who were really people, not rubber-stamps ; stories which, to a young literary beginner, were as fascinating as those of Grimm and Andersen had been to his childhood.

Some dark fairy must have been present at the birth of the 'nineties men of the Vigo Street group and some others of the time, and have breathed upon them some potent blight, so common among them was disaster or early death. Wilde fell into the pit he himself had dug. John Davidson drowned himself off the Cornish coast. Francis Adams died by his own hand at thirty. Hubert Crackanthorpe's body was taken from the Seine. Lionel Johnson died at thirty-five after a fall from one of those high stools used in public-houses. Stephen Phillips, after some years of golden prosperity, died in poverty in a one-room lodging. Francis Thompson was a homeless wanderer of the streets until rescued by the Meynells. Beardsley and Dowson died of tuberculosis, one at Mentone at twenty-six, the other, in Robert Sherard's lodgings at Catford, at thirty-one. A. C. Benson went into melancholy. William Watson received a knighthood but died forgotten and in poverty. Charles Conder lived and died a victim of Venus and Bacchus. Even the publishers of some of those men caught the blight from them. Leonard Smithers, after a prosperity permitting a house in Bedford Square, an office in Bond Street, a flat in Paris, a flat in Brussels, all running simultaneously, died at Fulham in a room furnished only with his death-bed, and was buried by the parish. Truly they were, as Yeats called them, The Tragic Generation.

" In order to be an artist," said the irresponsible Oscar, " it is first necessary to ruin one's health," and the young men of the 'nineties adopted an epigram as a maxim. Yet the epigram was not wholly facetious. It held a grain of truth : much good work in literature has been produced by invalids, and perhaps their enforced abstinence from physical activity was an aid to production. Keats, Thomas Hood, Heine, Carlyle, Harriet Martineau, Frank Smedley, Addington Symonds, Stevenson, and Beardsley are proof that robust health is not essential to the literary man. But they were constitutional invalids ; the others, by apathy or self-indulgence, reaped what they had sown in their dishevelled days and nights.

And during the nineteenth century they had many

forerunners. That century was strewn with wrecks. With most of them the cause was drink; the drink of that century having been of more fiery and mordant temper than the drink of this century which, if it has fewer geniuses, has fewer stories of wreckage. But there were others who lost their health with drugs, and set a fashion for the men of the 'nineties : Coleridge and De Quincey, with laudanum; Clarence Mangan, with laudanum and rum; Poe, with laudanum; Rossetti, with chloral; James Thomson, with laudanum and whisky; Francis Thompson, with laudanum; and Ernest Dowson followed them with experiments in hashish. They turned to drugs as a way out from physical pain or moral tedium, and they came into a dark kingdom whose climate coloured their work. In each case the work is charged with a sweet and potent spell not of this world. It holds the shadow of an unearthly life looming through an enchanted veil, which gives it such a power over the reader that it rings in the ear and the mind like a rune. That distillation of the white poppy produced such literary phenomena as *Kubla Khan* and *Christabel ; Ulalume* and *For Annie ; Dark Rosaleen* and *The Nameless One ;* the orchestral prose of *The English Mail Coach*, and the *Confessions ; The Hound of Heaven, The City of Dreadful Night,* and *Cynara*. But for their trespass into forbidden gardens those men had to pay a penalty, and common to all of them was a profound and torturing melancholy, the burden of remorse.

A few of the men of the Vigo Street 'nineties, the sensible and balanced, are still with us. They escaped the blight. Edwin Pugh, who lived to 1930, did not. He lived a life of almost constant penury, and his end was as grievous as that of Davidson and Crackanthorpe. In his later years his work ceased to be wanted, and he was living in a privation made just endurable by a Civil List pension of £100 a year when one morning he went out and did not return home. Enquiries were made, and after a day or two news came from a hospital that he had been found lying in the entry to a yard at Putney, unconscious, with injuries to head and face, as though he had been run over. In that hospital, where he lay unconscious for some days, he died, and a parish burial was only averted by a subscription made among a few fellow-authors by his good and patient friend, St. John Adcock.

Another ill-starred figure of that period whom I frequently saw about the Strand was the music-critic of one of the now-dead weeklies ; a brilliant music-critic too. Many a time I saw that distinguished man ordered out of Strand bars ; on one occasion in a very drastic and final manner. As he came into the bar the landlord gave him one look and pointed to the door. " It's no good coming in here. I'm not serving you. Outside. I don't mind a man getting tight in my house, but I won't have a man getting tight in someone else's house and coming here to be sick. Outside ! "

And there was yet another ill-starred man, who had died a few years earlier, in whom I was much interested ; not a man of the 'nineties but a straggler from the Pre-Raphaelite days. Pugh was the only man I knew who had met him.

Nobody pays much attention to the work of pavement artists or to the " artists " themselves, and probably nobody passing along Bayswater Road in the late 1890's gave more than a glance at a blotchy, unkempt screever and his coloured chalk drawings, or noticed that the drawings had an assured ease not usual in the work of screevers. But they would no doubt have given more than a glance if they had known that that screever had been hung in the Academy for twelve consecutive years and had been an admired friend of Burne-Jones, Walter Pater, and Swinburne. The screever was the almost legendary and now forgotten Simeon Solomon, whose name appears, always with epithets of compassion and regret, in many of the art and literary memoirs of the later nineteenth century.

He was born in Shoreditch in 1841. Drawing and painting came instinctively to him and to his elder brother Abraham who, after an Academy success, *Waiting for the Verdict*, at the age of sixteen, died at twenty-one. Simeon, after some study under his brother, entered the Royal Academy Schools at fifteen, and was first hung when he was seventeen. The subject of that first picture, like most of his subjects, was taken from the Old Testament, *The Finding of Moses*, and it won the cordial appreciation of Thackeray. He is described as at that time a handsome and graceful figure, with red hair, an exquisite profile, and brilliant eyes. His appearance alone made people notice him, and when his work was seen he won the applause of many of the alert, among them Swinburne and Pater ; while Burne-Jones, writing in later years in a perhaps over-generous mood, said, " Simeon Solomon was the greatest artist of us all."

Like many of the artists of that group he had a literary gift, and his little prose piece, *A Vision of Love Revealed in Sleep*, still sometimes turns up in second-hand catalogues. Written in an imitation of the more inflated manner of De Quincey, it records the wanderings of a spirit through a land where he sees the figure of Love in different stages of suffering caused by the wrongs and abuses inflicted by man. Something prophetic of himself in that. For Solomon didn't want his gifts or his personal beauty. He threw them to the dogs. The rot set in when he was about thirty. There are stories not only of drink but of drugs and sexual aberrations and abominations. A corrupt erotic element began to appear in his work. Also, it became coarse and careless in treatment, and he repeated himself. Friends warned him against prostituting his genius. He ignored them.

His aberrations in time became too extreme even

for the easy world of painters and writers. Men began to withdraw from him; his name began to be spoken only in a pitying murmur of dismissal. Swinburne not only broke with him but spoke of him as " a thing abhorrent to man, woman and beast." It appears that he and Swinburne had engaged in a somewhat bawdy correspondence, which Swinburne afterwards regretted, and that Solomon, hard-up, had been hawking Swinburne's letters around the West End dealers.

He had some fifteen years of success, prosperity and respect. Then he turned his back on it all, and deliberately lived the rest of his life as an exile among the lowest outcasts. He served a term in prison, but that didn't pull him up. His family got him into a mental home; that, too, was ineffectual. When he came out many efforts were made to reclaim him. He was set up with clothes, a studio, and a decent home. He sold the clothes and the furniture, and returned to the gutter. The decline and fall of a sensitive spirit is usually pitiful, but Solomon needed no pity. In his outcast state he was quite happy; he seemed indeed to take a chuckling delight in the freedom of rags and irresponsibility.

Most of his later years were spent as an inmate of the Holborn Workhouse, where, though he had lost all moral sense, he showed that he still had a good human feeling. When, by a few hastily-done drawings, he was able to raise a few shillings, he would take some of the old inmates out for the day and bring them back all comfortably tight. Somehow or other he supported that submerged and vagrant life for thirty years. He lingered on in drink and degradation, a ragged, decrepit old waif, till he was sixty-four ; till all those who had known him had forgotten him or presumed him dead. Then, one night in 1905, he was found, as Pugh years later was found, unconscious in the street. He was carried to his old home, the Holborn Workhouse, and in its infirmary he died.

None of those men had an atom of the Scotch vice

of hoarding. Money melted off them. It melted off
Pugh. But with none of them did it melt so swiftly
and magnificently as it melted off Oscar Wilde.
Robert Sherard told me many a tale of Wilde's
generosity—a generosity peculiar to him and of a rare
kind. Wilde was not a man, Sherard said, who would
share his last guinea with a friend. If it came to the
last guinea his egotism and self-interest made him hold
on to every shilling of it. But he would do something
much more unusual : he would share his prosperity.
Most men who would share their last crust with a
friend think twice about sharing when they possess
solid thousands ; they begin then to count and hold
on. Not so Oscar Wilde. Sherard told me that on
more than one occasion when he was hard-up, Wilde,
in his hours of affluence, would empty his pockets
and throw on the table clusters of fivers, tenners and
fifties, and say, " Help yourself, Robert. Do. Take
as much as you want. I've more than I need for the
moment."

Of his " needs " a friend of mine who was George
Alexander's secretary told me of a little incident in
which he was concerned at the St. James's Theatre.
One day at about noon, during the run of *The Importance of Being Earnest*, Wilde arrived at the theatre
and said he wanted a little money. My friend said,
" Yes, Mr. Wilde. Ten pounds ? Twenty ? "

" No, No," said Wilde. " Some *money*. Give me
a hundred."

So my friend gave him £100. At about half-past
eleven that evening, just as the theatre was closing,
Wilde again turned up, and explained that he was
taking one or two men to supper, and wanted a little
money. My friend reminded him that he had drawn
£100 that morning.

" Ah, yes. I know, my dear fellow, I know. But
I've spent that. Let me have another fifty."

In those early days of my acquaintance with Pugh
we had many long and pleasant wanderings up and

down London, and long and ardent talks on literature in the little Soho restaurants of that time. Before the film companies had invaded that quarter it was almost wholly a quarter of French, Italian and Swiss restaurants, and French and Italian *épiceries* and wine-shops. New restaurants opened every month or so, and each tried to outdo the other in the kind of *décor* that was thought to appeal to the English ; shaded lamps and discreet colour on each table, and walls of green and gold or primrose and vermilion or white and blue. But we preferred the simple places used by the men of the French or Italian colony. The cooking was bourgeois and the walls were plain whitewash, and the table-ware was thick. But cheap . . . ? They were unbelievable.

There were three places now vanished, one in Old Compton Street, one in Wardour Street, and one in Frith Street, which served for one shilling a light and satisfying dinner of four courses, *pain à discrétion*. Coffee was 2*d*. and a bottle of Graves 1*s*. There were a dozen places serving five-course dinners, coffee included, for 1*s*. 6*d*., and an Italian restaurant served a dinner of seven courses, including game in season, for 2*s*. 6*d*. Even at those places where you dined *à la carte*, your bill, whatever you had, seldom went above two shillings. Opposite a little 1*s*. 6*d*. table d'hôte in Soho Street, where we often met, was a one-room Turkish café to which we would adjourn to take Turkish coffee in a room with carpets on the walls and nothing on the floor, among a silent company playing backgammon. In Frith Street there was even a restaurant serving a table d'hôte of soup, meat-dish, vegetables, dessert, coffee and *pain à discrétion* at the dreamland price of 8*d*. At all those little places a bottle of *vin ordinaire* was 10*d*. All liqueurs were 6*d*., unless you took Chartreuse or Grand Marnier when you were stung for 9*d*.

Other cheap cafés of those days, now vanished, were the Dieppe, Au Petit Riche, the Franco-Suisse, and the Littoral—all in Soho. Also gone from other quarters are the Vienna, which stood at the corner of New Oxford Street and Hart Street ; the Marguerite, in Oxford Street ; the Gambrinus, Rupert Street ; Pratti's, in the Strand ; and the many Appenrodt restaurants. Restaurants of those days that had orchestras did not deafen us and compel our talk to be a series of staccato shouts. They gave us only discreet string-music ; not the howl and bark of Bill Blotz and his Blottos or Ike Hump and his Humpbacks, but bands that were Blue Hungarian or White Roumanian or Red Ziegeuner.

It was at those restaurants that I began to learn something about wine. Soho restaurants are not perhaps the best academy for a wine education, but they may serve as an elementary or prep. school. Anyway, they helped me to find my way among the simple beverage wines and to discover that my own taste was for the wines of the Rhine and the Moselle. And it has not changed. Above all the attractions of the wines of Bordeaux and Burgundy I prefer the Moselles and their bouquet of violets and moist earth, as light and gracious as a May morning, and the Hocks with their slightly heavier body and flinty flavour ; and I prefer them solus, not linked with food. For dessert wines and liqueurs I never cared, though among liqueurs I made many experiments and found that their chief interest was in their names. I have just turned out of my desk a liqueur-list of pre-1914. Out of that long array of liqueurs and cordials few can be had in the present war-years. Some of them we may not see in English restaurants for some years : Goldwasser, from Danzig ; Schnapps from Denmark ; Kümel, from Riga ; Maraschino, from Dalmatia ; Strega, from Italy ; Saké, from Japan ; Kirschwasser and Quetsch, from Alsace.

I began, too, to read on the subject of food and wine, and gathered a small shelf of books, most of which I still have to-day. Among them were Cyrus Redding's

Modern Wines; Doran's *Table Traits*, Walker's *Original*, with its papers on Aristology or the art of dining; Strauss's *Dishes and Drinks*; Dallas's *Book of the Table*; Blanchard Jerrold's *Cupboard Papers*; Edward Spencer's *Cakes and Ale*; Newnham-Davis's *Dinners and Diners*; Dr. Kitchiner's *Cook's Oracle*; Finck's *Foods and Flavours*; Abraham Hayward's *Art of Dining*; Launcelot Sturgeon's *Good Living*; Herman Senn's *Register of Dishes* and Brillat-Savarin's *Physiologie du Goût*. The last is everywhere accepted as a classic of gastronomy, but I prefer Thomas Walker and Abraham Hayward. Brillat-Savarin's book is not the book of an epicure. He was not gourmet but gourmand, and the long meals he describes with such gusto belong not to men of taste but to guzzlers. So do those described by Thackeray with such parade of taste in his gastronomical papers; they appeal only to gluttons. Walker was the true epicure. He was the first advocate of the small dinner—three well-chosen and balanced dishes, served without display on a table without needless decoration and without servants to hand round the minor dishes. All minor dishes and wines and condiments, he held, should be on the table within reach of the guests.

Somewhere about that time, since it is linked in my mind with Soho restaurants and my first bottle of Moselle, I issued my first book or booklet—twenty-five copies, privately printed, of a selection of my verses, which I called, because I couldn't think of any other title, *Verses*. It was kindly received by the papers whose opinion in any way mattered—I sent it only to six—but I valued more than what they said about the verses themselves their general comment. Which, from *The Times Literary Supplement*, the *Athenæum* and the *Bookman*, was to the effect that the verses, while of no particular account, showed that I had the root of the matter in me and gave promise of something to come. The booklet also brought me kind letters from A. C. Benson, Herbert

Trench, Clement Shorter, " E. Nesbit," Edward
Thomas, St. John Adcock and one or two others,
which again I valued not for what the writers said
but for their taking the trouble to say it. It also
brought me their acquaintance and that of some other
of my seniors.

I found E. Nesbit, who was then living at the old
manor-house of Well Hall, at Eltham, as I had expected from her books to find her, a darling. Her
husband, Hubert Bland, had not her gift of easy
friendliness and happy-go-lucky style. He affected
rather the aloof attitude ; detached and reserved.
Seeing him sitting by the fire in dinner dress, with his
white hair, his monocle with its broad black ribbon,
and his high-pitched, drawling voice, I could hardly
believe he was real. He was so much the Old Squire
that he seemed to be one of the photographic paint-
ings of Dendy Sadler. Both of them were Socialists
and members of the Fabian Society, and both of
them, in evening clothes, entertained young Socialist
workers.

Clement Shorter, another acquaintance I made,
had at that time considerable influence in the literary
world. It was said that a good notice of a book by
him in his weekly Literary Letter in the *Sphere* would
by itself sell five hundred copies of any book. He
had his oddities, and it is always a man's oddities
that attract me. I have little interest in those who
have smoothed away the obstreperous wrinkles of
their character and flattened their salients. I prefer
always those with twists and angles and foibles. He
had a number of little vanities, and a habit of laying
down the law on literature, and when he didn't like
a book he could not believe that other people could
really like it.

But he was a genuine bookman (one sign of your
genuine bookman is given by the way he takes a book
into his hands) and he had a passion for literature,
and for this many little asperities may be disregarded.

As a bookman he was, perhaps, more genuine than his great friend of whom he was often talking, the bibliophile Thomas J. Wise, whose enthusiasm for privately printed editions was so intense that it was eventually the cause of that entertaining book, Carter and Pollard's *An Enquiry Into the Nature of Certain Nineteenth-Century Pamphlets*; which, in its turn, was the cause of much embarrassment to Thomas J. Wise and others.

Many unkind stories used to be told of Clement Shorter. He was sensitive to supposed slights or sneers, and had a gift for making enemies and for keeping them. In his Literary Letter one would often see certain flicks and fleers at unnamed people whom from private knowledge one could name as long-cherished offenders against the Shorter etiquette. Three of the regular objects of these flicks were Grant Richards, Edmund Gosse and Arthur Waugh. Most of the stories told about him are too unkind to circulate; I always found Shorter himself most kind. But perhaps two of them, being so ludicrously far-fetched, are harmless enough. The story of the Patagonian prince and princess, who were expected at a garden-party, but became victims of the English climate and couldn't attend; and the surprise of the hostess when some of her guests spoke of the prince and princess, and how well they understood English, which puzzled her until she saw on the lawn Mr. and Mrs. Clement Shorter. And the story, turning on Shorter's dark complexion and curly hair, of a friend of Shorter's stoutly denying the legend that Shorter was Jewish, and saying that he strongly objected to being thought of as a Jew, to which somebody retorted, " Of course. Any nigger would."

I remember clearly my first meeting with W. H. Davies. I remember my first meeting with most people, whether poets or pedlars, artists or artisans, novelists or nobodies. I am not like that man whose book of recollections, published in 1863, must, if he

ever saw it, have horrified Browning. In a famous
lyric Browning cried, " Ah, did you once see Shelley
plain, And did he stop and speak to you ? " Well,
Cyrus Redding, in his *Yesterday and To-Day*, writes
of his friendship with Leigh Hunt, and of the people
he met around Hunt when Hunt was living at the
Vale of Health, Hampstead ; and adds, as a casual
afterthought : " I imagine I once met Shelley at his
house, but I met so many I forget most of their names."
A remark that makes one anxious, like Charles Lamb
on another occasion, to feel the gentleman's bumps.

Davies was then living at the Weald, Sevenoaks.
It was before he became an incomplete townsman
at Great Russell Street and later at Avery Row. But
it was in town that I first met him. His reputation
was then in the making, but he was already sure of
himself and of his way. The chief memory I took
from that first brief meeting was of his soft, clear
eyes and the upward, bird-like turn of his face in talk ;
and of his dress—a coat of one material and colour, the
trousers of another, and the waistcoat of a third. His
tailors were, I imagine, Marks and Spencer, but somehow the outfit was for him just right. We met in
the street, and he stood and talked for half an hour
in the buffeting crowd, with as much detachment as
though we had met at one of his quiet country cross-
roads. In character he was at once simple and shrewd ;
innocent and wide-awake ; gentle and inflexible ;
modest but never humble.

When he settled in town I saw him often at Great
Russell Street and at Avery Row, off Bond Street,
and many a time I would see him at lonely spots in
remote parts of London, standing and staring. In
Great Russell Street he had three rooms over a grocer's
shop and lived in only one of them. At Avery Row
there was but one, and getting into that room was a
business. When he opened the door he had to retire
from it ; it opened, with an inch or two to spare,
on to the wash-stand. So Davies had to retire, and

you had to edge yourself in and slide between the wash-stand and the bed, to close the door, and then slide between the bed and the table to a chair in the corner.

It was difficult to believe that this soft-voiced, gentle-mannered poet had ever been a hobo, tramping the States and jumping freight-trains ; especially difficult in face of his fussiness and old-maid precision in quite trivial matters, such as the habits of the woman next door or the landlady's cat or making an appointment. If you were arranging to call on him there would be a palaver about it. " Then that's fixed," he would say in his slow, soft, deliberate voice ; " you'll come along on Wednesday at four o'clock. If for any reason you can't come, you'll let me know by Tuesday. And if for any reason I have to alter it, *I'll* let *you* know by Tuesday. So if *you* don't hear from *me* by Tuesday, you'll come along. And if *I* don't hear from *you* by Tuesday, I'll expect you. That's quite clear, isn't it ? "

Very different from the gentle soft-eyed poet was a man I met in the same week ; a writer who became world-famous. He had just then had his first novel published, and already he looked successful, flushed with success, bouncing with it. He had, it seemed to me, set out to cultivate material and professional success for its own sake, and he planned for it, laid foundations for it, dressed for it, talked for it, assumed it before he had solidly attained it. I have heard him speak of his early literary struggles. He had none. I have heard him say he knew what poverty was. He never did. He knew nothing like the hardships and frustrations experienced by young writers with none of his social connections and other backing. His literary life from the beginning was all velvet. He came to London with what he called the miserable allowance of thirty shillings a week, at that time equal to the five pounds of to-day, which gave security whatever he earned. He had also a good wardrobe and good introductions, and soon after his arrival he was reviewing for a leading morning paper—work which many men with equal equipment sought in vain.

I never knew a man so quickly and with so small an output establish himself as he did after about two books. Not content to let his distinguished work make its way on its own merits, as such work would in any case have done, he pushed it along with all he had. He had obviously noted the advantage of Being In with the Right People, and he set out to make the acquaintance and win the friendship of every famous figure of the current literary scene. Everything was used for Success ; the lunch-party, the dinner-table, the drawing-room, the Society function, the literary function, the lecture platform—all were for him appliances for the building of Success. For so generous and gifted a man this poor ambition, and the means by which he nursed it, seemed to me ridiculous, and though I later perceived that his desire to surround himself with a wall of success and sympathetic friends, and to be always in the procession, was only a cover for a quite amiable and understandable weakness, my very slight acquaintance with him stayed where it was.

A more pleasant acquaintance of that time was an unassuming artist of the 'nineties—Edgar Wilson, who had been one of the men who made the old comic weekly, *Pick-Me-Up*, which was noted not so much for its " comic " letterpress, which was feeble, but very much for its drawings. Wilson had then more or less ceased work, and was living in the suburb adjoining mine, and making a collection of Japanese art. Among the treasures he showed me was the private sketch-book of Hokusai. I had seen some of Beardsley's unpublished and suppressed drawings, and I had seen some of the horrors offered secretly in Brussels and Paris, but I had not and never have seen such bizarre obscenities as some of the sketches in that book, nor such exquisite work devoted to such stuff. I have often wondered what happened to that book after his death. His own work had something of the Japanese quality (the normal Japanese quality) ; it may be seen in the head-pieces and tail-pieces he did for *Pick-Me-Up* and the *Pall Mall Magazine* and the *Butterfly* ; and I still have two or three etchings of his which he pulled for me on his press a week or so before he died ; etchings of London riverside subjects.

Studying with unsophisticated eyes the authors I met in those early years I noted a point that surprised me. They were all of one profession, yet they had nothing in common. Each was distinct in appearance, manner and dress. In other professions, medicine, law, commerce, men, in appearance at least, run to type. There is a legal face, a doctor's face, a business face, a military face, a sea face, acquired by all men engaged in those callings. But there is no literary face, no type which all authors somewhere touch. Take any group of professional writers at a public literary lunch or dinner, and nobody could guess what they were or what they had in common. If they guessed at all they would guess that this one was a lawyer, that one a business-man, the other an actor, and yet another a clerk or a shop-keeper or a labourer. The reason is, of course, that the arts are not an all-time profession. A man may devote to them the whole of his inner being but only part of his time. They are not one of life's constant activities ; they are a source of life. You cannot compel them to bring forth every day and all day. And since every artist is a unique being, and the practice of an art is a calling to which a man is drawn solely by his singular and individual character, for which he seeks expression, he may be a member or ex-member of some other profession, and come from any one of the numerous social classes, and be so strongly himself as to receive no impress from the practice of his art. "Where," said a woman to her hostess at a reception at which

Browning was beaming and gossiping away to a small circle, " where did you find that very exuberant bank-manager ? "

In those days authors, with a few exceptions such as Shaw, Wells and Chesterton, were authors only, concerned for the most part with life in its larger aspects and with the problems of their art, and scarcely at all with such academic detail as the grey business of government and politics and economics. To-day, most authors have become vociferous experts on blue-prints and plans for New Worlds, and litter their works with such lifeless terms as ideology and racial frontiers and subsistence-levels and distributism and co-ordination and gold-standard. I wonder why they should feel called upon to plunge thus into subjects that need a lifetime of study for their full understand-ing, and are not, for authors, their province. Wells, who was once the delight of those of us who are middle-aged, long ago took leave of his Comic Muse and his Fantastic Muse, and entered that gritty world. Chesterton, after leading us up the garden with *The Napoleon of Notting Hill*, *Manalive* and *The Flying Inn*, started a weekly paper. We all thought it would be carried on in the uproarious, ten-sizes-larger-than-life spirit of those books. And what did he do but fill it with dreary trade stuff about guilds and dis-tributism and what not. Stuff of that sort from the man who had made *The Man Who Was Thursday*, and who knew how you went to Birmingham by way of Beachy Head.

Our poets too have renounced their true office and now occupy themselves with the ephemeral and vul-gar topics which serve platform men and debating societies ; such things as the horrid results of indus-trialism and mass-life in towns and the moral and political evils of these times. Why do they do it ? Do they think these barren things more real than the imagined splendours and conflicts of which men have made literature ? Surely the spiritual sunshine afforded by the literature of any century does more for man's true growth than five centuries of political pamphlets and social reform. How much have the devisers of Utopian worlds added to the sum of human happiness compared to that given by the poets and romancers? There is nothing creative in the mission of sociology; no sunshine or sustenance for the soul.

Social and political wrongs were widely discussed in the days of Keats and Shelley and Wordsworth. Keats went on being a poet. Shelley and Wordsworth felt that they ought to do something about those wrongs—and did. But the result was never poetry. Dickens allowed himself to be agitated by the thought of social injustice and political corruption, and actually thought that *Pickwick* and *Oliver Twist* and *Nicholas Nickleby* had special virtue because they helped to abolish debtors' prisons and harsh Poor Laws and bad schools. But for one thing they didn't abolish imprisonment for debt or Bumbles or ill-managed schools; and for another, nobody to-day cares twopence whether they abolished social wrongs or not. They did something more positive than abolition. They created a world of fantasy in whose streets and among whose people we can wander with delight, and they gave new exercise to the god-like faculty of laughter.

The concern of the artist with these matters is scarcely ever of much service. Not all their speeches and pamphlets and propaganda put together do as much towards the setting right of men's hearts as a perfect lyric or some revelation of the significance of this life and man's place in the divine harmony of which it is a part. Greater exultation has been caused in the hearts of men by *Lycidas* or the Choral Symphony than by the grant of an eight-hour day or the Factory Acts or Council Houses. Charles Chaplin's early films, lightly thrown out of a sympathetic imagination, did more to inspire people with goodwill to their fellows than all the propaganda issued by the social reformers. *David Copperfield* has surely been the cause of more delight than Unemployment Insurance or Free Medical Service. More people have had their horizons widened and their lives enriched by reading the Shakespeare sonnets or *Epipsychidion* or *Faust* than by hearing of some social-justice scheme for better housing conditions and higher wages.

When the Spanish civil war was raging some years ago Miss Nancy Cunard sent out a questionnaire to a number of novelists, poets and artists on what they felt about the conflict and where their sympathies lay. We were compelled, she said, to take sides : in these times nobody could stand out in ironic detachment. Most of us were caught by the question and answered it one way or another. Only some half-dozen made the sensible answer—that there are more important things in the world than ephemeral political movements and creeds, and that the artist, as an individualist, is concerned with preserving his personal relationship to the eternal values of life and with showing their value to all men ; not with the fluctuating trivia of governments.

Wagner's creed, even in these days, is worth remembering : " I believe in God, Mozart and Beethoven, and in their disciples and apostles. I believe in the Holy Ghost and the truth of art. I believe that this art proceeds from God and dwells in the hearts of all enlightened men. I believe that all men may become blest through this art."

The best service that artists can give their fellows to-day is that given by the artists of the past—to go on with their work, undisturbed by the outer upheavals ; to concentrate on the spiritual and emotional side of man's life. The mere act of concentrating on these things starts a wave which can reach to the ends of the earth and vibrate through centuries of time, and bring man a far greater blessing than political freedom or garden-cities. The concentration which produced the *Morte d'Arthur*, *The Pilgrim's Progress*, *Gargantua and Pantagruel*, *The Magic Flute*, *Tristan*, *The Tempest*, and works which each of us can name to himself, is not yet spent. Human lives are still affected by these works in a way beyond the power of any expedients of science or sociology. They came from men of goodwill and they reach to the roots of our being ; roots which no war or political or social upheaval can ever disturb. They move the Dweller in our Innermost as no prospect of Utopia or New Atlantis can move him.

Some of our novelists may have valuable political ideas which, if put into operation, might lead to the abolition of many horrid features of our daily life. Yet whatever, for example, H. G. Wells may have given to the world in this way, none of it balances a *Kipps*, a *Mr. Polly* or a *Tono-Bungay*. Man does not live by social security alone, and however valuable J. B. Priestley's ideas may be on Reconstruction and Social Justice, he will not be as blest for them as he has been for *The Good Companions* and *Angel Pavement*. It is the office of the poets and the artists and the novelists to show us the real life that each of us lives behind the screen of common daily routine. Those other matters may be left to men expert in them.

.   .   .   .   .   .

During those early years of literary life I was still living in my old suburb but we had moved from Geneva Street to somewhat better rooms. The rooms were over a confectioner's shop, and the front room looked out upon a little half-circle that made one of those backwater villages which were a feature of that suburb. Within fifty yards of my window I had a combined baker's and Post Office, a grocer, a fruiterer, a public-house and off-licence, a butcher, a tobacconist, a draper, a newsagent, a household store, a laundry, an ironmonger, a chemist and a delicatessen shop. A self-contained community indeed, quite independent

o

of the High Street, and with its own exuberant
Saturday Night and its own adagio Sunday.   The
byway was even a bus-route ; a minor service ran
through it, linking our suburb with two others to the
west of it, and lending the street the air of a highway
and of busy-ness.   The public-house served not only as
a public-house but as a regular pitch for street-organs
and other wandering music, and I was daily and nightly
entertained by organ, clarinet, harp, accordion and
guitar, and not at all entertained by an incompetent
cornet.

In looking back to the homes of our youth memory
seldom works on the material active life we led in
them ; it works almost wholly on the mental and
interior life ; and that street-scene is for me the setting not of my daily life at that time, and the things
I was doing, but of my long, wild-ranging thoughts
and hopes and reveries ; the new tracts of literature
and music I was discovering and the stories I was
inventing.

Often I wished for more seemly surroundings, and
sometimes I had visions of the elegant kind of flat
and the properly furnished study I would have in
central London if ever I got to the position of being
able to drive up to my editors or publishers or agents
in a taxi or my own car, as I often saw Zangwill and
Conan Doyle and Stanley Weyman doing.   But then
some idea for a story would seize me, and I would
forget those dreams and our out-of-date furniture
and lack of fittings in the glow of an interest richer
and keener than any that could be given by a fine
flat and study and other possessions.   And I know
now that I could have had no better setting for what
I was doing ; almost every glance out of the window
picked up the germ of a story, and on three occasions,
when guitar and clarinet music was coming up to my
window out of the dark, I was moved to write a poem
to my little suburb ; poems that appeared, I think,
in the *Nation*.   Many an evening at twilight, with

raindrops falling before the lighted shop-windows and turning from pearl to topaz, and the sky still light, and the mist rising, I would look out at that scene, and would be thinking, say, of a passage of De Quincey and of some crystal aria of the angelic Gluck ; and all those things—the evening, the street-scene, the rain, the homely little shops and shoppers, and the De Quincey passage and the aria—would fuse and make one work whose quality would pour and tingle through all my nerves, and fill the street and the evening and my own heart with a bliss that I can recapture at this moment but never can convey.

Suburban it may have been, but since the majority of London's people lives in suburbs, the suburban streets are as highly charged with essence of London as Trafalgar Square or Oxford Street. As a son of London I knew this and could respond to it. London was my city. It was in my bones and my blood, and part of my work, I knew, would be an attempt to re-present its life, and an important part of that life was to be found in suburbs like my own. I had read all the writers on London who had touched London Scenes, from the Elizabethans up to Wilfred Whitten, and I had noted the odd fact that few of them were Londoners. With the exception of Dekker, Stow, Defoe and Lamb, all those identified in the public mind with the literary pageant of London came from outside. Pepys was from Cambridgeshire, Addison from Wiltshire, Steele from Dublin, Johnson from Lichfield, Richardson from Derby, Boswell from Scotland ; and of the others, Pierce Egan, Dickens, Thackeray, Walter Besant, George Gissing, Pett Ridge, Jerome, Wilfred Whitten, none was London-born. London gave England some of its chief singers—Chaucer, Spenser, Milton, Donne, Cowley, Gray, Blake, Keats, Browning, Swinburne—but they made no song of their native soil ; they turned rather to rural themes and left the celebration of their city to the settlers from the counties.

None of these quite satisfied me in their pictures and interpretations. They saw London mainly as a material and spiritual spectacle ; they looked at it from the outside. It was not, as with Londoners, part of their bones and blood, nor were they part of it. It was the difference between being a gypsy and being George Borrow ; Borrow might have seen more varieties of gypsy life than any one gypsy saw, but the gypsy was the life and Borrow was not. So the Londoners, who were reproved by the glowing commentators from the provinces for taking their city for granted and for not visiting the Abbey and the Tower and St. Paul's, smilingly admitted the charge and instead of looking at London went on being part of it.

. . . . .

I was not at that time submitting my MSS for approval. I was suggesting subjects and receiving definite commissions to write, but living, as I had to, on the caprices of editors, there were periods when things were strained. Sometimes there was no money, and sometimes things were strained even when I had money. There was an occasion when I had a cheque for a story and yet went hungry for some days because I could not cash it. I had not then achieved a bank account, and I usually got Edwin Pugh to pass my cheques through his bank. But on that occasion he had gone to the country for one of those long week-ends—Thursday to Thursday—and I was left with several guineas on paper and one-and-eightpence in cash. I lived seven days on that one-and-eightpence, and for months afterwards I recoiled from the sight of a banana.

Sometimes there was no cash and no cheque, and then I had to sell off some of my books. There was a time when I had a Meredith fever and was flushed with *Love in the Valley*, *Phœbus with Admetus* and *Modern Love* and *The Lark Ascending*, and since I had not the nerve to write to the Olympian I felt that I must go to Dorking and distantly pay my respects by looking at the famous Flint Cottage. But there was no money for the fare, so I sold a bundle of books, all first editions, mainly of Wilde. I sold *The Happy Prince, The Ballad of Reading Gaol, An Ideal Husband, A Woman of No Importance, A House of Pomegranates*; and Aubrey Beardsley's *Under the Hill*, Sherard's privately printed *Story of an Unhappy Friendship* (the book through which I had made his acquaintance) and Gissing's *Henry Ryecroft* and Butler's *Way of all Flesh*. The bookseller to whom I took them gave me sixteen shillings for the lot. When I think what those first editions would fetch to-day . . .

Still, with what they fetched I made my pilgrimage to Dorking, and stood for about an hour at a respectful distance from the cottage, in the hope that I might catch a glimpse of him. I didn't. But the mere sight of the walls and chimneys of his dwelling set up within me such vibrations as one might receive from the sight of the burning bush ; and the fact that, as I learned some years later, I had been all the time standing outside the wrong cottage could not then rob me of the devout thrills I had experienced. I never did see him. But as some sort of compensation I more than once saw Swinburne striding up Putney Hill, and at a Tooting villa I met a white-haired and venerable figure for whose christening Mendelssohn, when staying at Herne Hill, had composed his *Spring Song*; and in the High Street of Eltham I saw the elusive and almost-invisible underwriter-novelist, "Seton Merriman."

In those hand-to-mouth times I was often annoyed by the prophecy, made by all sorts of people, of better times coming to me. It was not one here and there ; they all said it ; and though I pressed them for evidence, being unable myself to see any, and though they could give none, they went on saying it. One or two of them said it, not from seeing any of my work but after a single meeting with me. How they could say it of anybody so unthrusting as myself, I don't know ; nor did they. They only said, "You'll be all right. You've plenty of success before you." But I scorned their prophecies, and assumed that either they were talking into the air or were being polite. But their unanimity was as surprising as the assurance with which they spoke, as though speaking from the subconscious. Arthur Waugh was always saying it ; I still have one or two facetious verses he wrote me on the subject. William Heinemann said it, but though he pronounced my first collection of short stories a good collection he wouldn't publish it. Edwin Pugh said it. E. Nesbit said it. Norman Douglas said it. Edward Thomas said it. It annoyed me because comfort in the future, even if it happened (and the idea was fantastic) was no balm to present discontents and makeshifts. The only man with whom I agreed was Robert Sherard who said he couldn't see any sort of promise in my work or any hope for me in what he called the Literary Arena. (He knew all the clichés, and used them lovingly.)

But Sherard always talked of literary life as though it were some sort of mêlée or wrestling-match. I never could see it as any kind of competition, and anyway I never could compete or struggle. I never " struggled for recognition " or tried to draw attention to myself. I just did my work. But he was, I think, a rather disappointed man who had had a few backhanders in his career, and had not enough protective covering of humour to take them with resilience. I remember his telling me of a backhander he received (unmeant) from George Gissing. He was returning to France, his regular home, and at Charing Cross, from which the boat-train then started, he met a friend. The friend had Gissing with him. They were introduced, and Gissing said, " Oh—Robert Sherard, is it ? I've wanted to meet you for *so long*." Most of us, however modest, have a spark of vanity which will glow to such a remark, and Sherard duly glowed. Until Gissing continued, " You knew Daudet, and I've so much wanted to meet somebody who knew him."

There is a certain West End bookshop where authors are frequently in peril of backhanders. Authors' faces are not so well known as those of actors and athletes and politicians, and on two or three occasions I have seen authors at that shop in situations which the old comic papers would have described as Collapse of Author. I was there one morning when Maurice Hewlett was present. Some assistant, near by, was attending to a customer, and offered a new book of Hewlett's. The customer, a woman, said, " No, thank you. Hewlett wrote that lovely thing, *The Forest Lovers*. When he'd written that he should have died." Another time I was standing near E. V. Lucas, when a man and a woman, next to us, were ranging over the newest-book counter, and the man picked up a volume of Lucas essays, and said, " What about this ? " The woman said, " Lord, no. I can't stand Charles Lamb. I certainly can't stand Lamb-and-water." And I saw Jerome get one. He was hovering about when an assistant, attending to a most elegant young man, who might have been Ronald Firbank but I think was not, said, " Here's a new volume of sketches by Jerome." " Thank you," the young man said, " but I don't care for books written with a mouth-organ on a Bank Holiday."

An almost daily associate of mine at one time was a writer little known to the general public, but a writer of considerable quality—Cranstoun Metcalfe. He was the author of two novels, *Splendid Mourning* and *Peaceable Fruit*, and a volume of quiet, reflective essays published anonymously, *The Lowly Estate*, and was when I knew him reader for the publisher Andrew Melrose, another man who thought my first collection of stories was good but wouldn't publish it. Metcalfe was a man of great personal charm, of gentle temper and, despite many hardships, constant good humour.

He had a particular pleasure in ridiculous stories ;
the more ridiculous they were the more he liked them ;
and he was much given to projecting facetious titles
for novels, as *The Poet's Daughter, or She was not
Averse ; The Pipes of Pan, or the W. Cerial ; The
Secret Chamber, or the Mystery of Edgar Allan ; The
Ghostly Derelict, or The Smack that never Reached the
Bottom.*   On the subject of titles he often remarked
on the public's misapprehension of a title, as in the
well-known cases of *Lorna Doone* and *Notes on the
Construction of Sheepfolds*, and liked to point out to
people who hadn't noticed it how, in certain chemists'
shops of Praed Street and Villiers Street, Joseph
McCabe's sober and serious work, *Twelve Years in a
Monastery*, is always set next to *The Awful Confessions
of Maria Monk.*

A story he particularly relished was that of a friend
of his whose landlord threatened that unless the last
two quarters' rent was paid he would take legal proceedings to recover ; whereupon the tenant wrote
back and threatened proceedings against the landlord for demanding money with menaces.   And a
story of a man sitting next to him at a theatre where a
young actor, a newly-arrived West End star, was presenting *Hamlet*.   After the second act the man turned
to Metcalfe and gave a snort. " Huh. Fancy that
young fellow having the cheek to play Hamlet. Why,
I knew his father ! "   And another story of a man he
knew who had friends named Blackwell, Gilbert,
Fletcher, Weare and Webb, and looked about for
introductions to five other men of particular names,
and, after much search and contrivance, found them,
and then gave a lunch-party at the Café Royal and
paired off his guests—Crosse and Blackwell, Gilbert
and Sullivan, Thurtell and Weare, Beaumont and
Fletcher, and Mappin and Webb.   And another of
the shopkeeper who came away from a trade dinner
with the wrong hat and, thinking he knew whose hat
it was, and wishing to put the matter right, and in a

dignified way, he sent the man a third-person note, "Mr. Brown presents his compliments to Mr. Jones, and he has a hat which isn't mine. If Mr. Jones has a hat which isn't yours, I shouldn't be surprised if they are the ones."

He was always bubbling with these facetiæ, and would let them out as we were walking up Fleet Street or striving against the press of the Strand. They went not inaptly with his austere pinched face, his scholarly mind and his gracious silver melancholy.

.   .   .   .

In 1913 and 1914, the last years of the old and benighted though moderately sensible world in which my first twenty-seven years were spent, there was a certain restlessness in the air. Outwardly the scene and the social temper were as they had been. London still had German *bier-halles* and German restaurants. The tops of buses were still uncovered from the wind and the rain. Men still in summer wore straw hats ; hansoms and four-wheelers were still about ; and public-houses still kept open till half an hour after midnight. A few features of the scene were special to those years. Smart young men were called Nuts, and smart young women wore skirts slashed up one side to show the leg. A novelty of the time was the fashion-parade of mannequins held at restaurants and theatre matinées. The tango had arrived from Argentina, and the smart hotels were holding Tango Teas. But the tango was difficult, and the waltz was still the favourite dance, and was drawing new life from waltzes of the time—*Septembre, Automne, Destiny, Nights of Gladness*. Those who couldn't manage the tango but wanted something new turned to the new American thing—the fox-trot. *Parsifal* had had its first performance at Covent Garden in despite of Wagner's solemn decree that it should never be done outside Bayreuth ; George Edwardes had abandoned musical comedy for Viennese opera ; the Alhambra

was making a feature of revue, at some distance from
the French form ; and America had set the town
alight with new rhythms. *Hullo, Ragtime* had packed
the Hippodrome ; *Come Over Here* was packing the
Kingsway Opera House, and street-boys were whistling
the *Gaby Glide* and *Hitchy Koo* and *Waiting for the
Robert E. Lee* ; and Sir Thomas Beecham gave London
its first intoxicating experience of Russian opera with
Chaliapin and Russian Ballet with Nijinsky.

But everywhere the restless spirit was perceptible,
as of people waiting on some impending climax.
Nobody knew that we had reached the end of an age,
yet everybody in his bones and blood was sensible of
something disconcerting, some hovering and pervading
disquiet. I was myself sensible of it, but I gave it
little notice since I was involved during those two
years in a personal and private distress. The event of
my life had just then happened, and it was for me a
time when I went on living without reason or purpose,
with my faculties only at half-pressure, myself an
organism going through undirected and unrealised
perfunctory motions ; a time when all the good things
of life, even literature and music, had lost their savour
and appeal, and my whole horizon and everything
that was had resolved themselves into one face and one
name.

When at last I came out of that fog, my affairs
began to change for the better. Commissions became
fairly frequent, and I was no longer put to the pain of
making the post a morbid centre of my day. In my
teens it had been my habit always to be out at about
the time of the last post—nine o'clock—and not to
return until about half-past when I would know at
once whether there was or was not something for me.
That was done to avoid the trepidation of waiting, of
hearing the postman approach door by door, of wondering whether there would be anything, whether he was
going to knock at our door or to pass ; and then of
hearing him next door, and waiting some seconds, and

realising at last that he had passed, and there was nothing, nothing ; or of hearing him pause, and then hearing the rattle of the letter-box ; and then the breathless few seconds of descent, wondering whether it would be This or That ; and then seeing a foolscap envelope and knowing at last with a clouded heart that it was That.

There was an end to that nonsense. Editors were becoming well disposed. My work was appearing in the more serious things—the *English Review*, the *New Witness*—and I was kept agreeably occupied. Publishers, too, were showing interest. One day I found in my desk the manuscript of that collection of short stories, and as I was slowly resuming an interest in things I thought I would give it one more airing, and then, if it didn't this time find a friend, destroy it. The stories had some sort of unity in their setting. They were stories about the Chinese in the docks quarter of London, and I called them *Limehouse Nights*. At the time I did them I had no knowledge of the Chinese people, and all I knew of Limehouse and the district was what I had automatically observed without aim or purpose during my unguided wanderings in remote London. I had thus been able to write those stories with the peculiar assurance a man has who knows nothing of what he is writing or talking about.

On this which was to be in any case their last journey they did find a friend, and almost at the same time I received a commission from George Allen & Unwin to write a book for them. That book, published a few months before *Limehouse Nights*, became my first book, *Nights in Town*. One's first book is always easily done, and *Nights in Town* which, as first published, was a book of about 90,000 words, was done in about ten weeks. This does not mean that it was rushed ; only that, because it was a first book, it did not present the problem that later books present. The reason why a first book is easily done, and why it usually has a zest and freshness and wealth of character and incident and observation not often present in later work, is that one has a clear field in which to move, no obstacles in the shape of previous books to turn one aside and fill one with apprehensions of repeating oneself.

Before *Nights in Town* I had published two privately-printed booklets of verse, and had done five or six anthologies for various publishers, work which by my long and widely-assorted reading came easily to me. But with *Nights in Town* I had at last accomplished something solid that was wholly mine. I had a full-length book of my own to my credit, and I could write my name as " Author of . . ." and experience a thrill never to be experienced again. I had become what I had wanted to be. To-day, after forty years in or on the edge of the literary world, I can say that all that those authors told me about it when trying to dissuade me from making it my livelihood was correct. I have experienced all the conditions expressed by the terms they used—and I have been quite happy in them. It was the life I desired, the natural life for me, and once you have found and can follow your right career it brings satisfactions of its own against which success or failure, prosperity or penury, are minor matters to which you give no thought.

Nights in Town, when it appeared at the opening of the war-to-end-war, was generously noticed, and was in demand in one or other of its several impressions for twenty-five years. The volume of short stories also had a pleasant reception from the critics both here and in America, and had also an immediate modest success with the public of both countries, and has been selling for twenty-eight years. Both books brought me an extraordinary number of letters, especially the volume of stories. I found that many readers of these, knowing nothing of the nature or processes of authorship, took it for granted that I had lived the kind of grim life shadowed in the stories. They do not, of course, bear the slightest relation to my actual life. My life has been, as these pages show, a quiet, commonplace literary man's life, and its circumstances those of everyday ; nothing in the least romantic or odd or adventurous. Yet those outside the world of writers, knowing little of the possibilities of imagination, persist in thinking that stories of that kind could not have been written without first-hand knowledge, and persist in picturing me, to their disappointment when meeting me, as a big husky fellow accustomed to knocking about in the tough corners of the world—a sort of Jack London. Whereas I am indeed much nearer to the cartoonist's John Citizen.

When that book of stories had been out for three or four months, and was showing signs of selling, I got hard up. So I went to the publisher and asked him if he would cancel the royalty agreement and give me fifty pounds for the copyright and all rights. He said he wouldn't. I said I would be much obliged if he would. He said he was sure I wouldn't later on be obliged ; I'd be sorry. I said I was sure I wouldn't ; what you've never had you never miss, they say, and I quickly forget my business mistakes. But he wouldn't do it. I sat and sat, repeating my plea, and he stood and stood, repeating his refusal, and as I haven't a great deal of endurance I tired before he did. Bless him.

. . . . . .

As I stood in reverie in that Bond Street gallery with my eyes on that Kate Greenaway picture, and my mind on the scenes of years ago, I saw its pinks and greens dissolve into my own first box of crayons, and I saw the High Street of my suburb and its side-streets, and I saw Geneva Street in springtime, and its long front gardens of nasturtium and fuchsia and mignonette, and I saw it on winter evenings when it was a little canal of twilight and street-lamps and lit windows, with the twilight at once the soul of the scene and the spectator of it.

None of us really grows up. Before the elemental

things of life, before the earth and the sea and the stars, before night and morning, birth and death and love, all of us are on a level ; child, adult, scholar and peasant can only stand stilled and wondering. Nothing is real, says Berlioz, except what takes place in that little corner of our being called the heart. It is there that our real lives are lived, and external event, however it ruffles the outer life, is no more than wind on the surface of the water. In the heart nothing changes. We pass through life and acquire experience, and become more sensible, more rational, more able to meet the daily occasions of life and their problems, but those matters are merely of the mind. The things we learn are of no importance. What is important is what we know in our hearts, and what we fully know at forty or fifty or sixty is what we knew when we were six. That is the only knowledge we need ; the knowledge we brought with us ; the only knowledge that is ever really ours. Each life is only a development through experience towards a full comprehension of that knowledge.

And what I know in my heart to-day is what I knew at that first remembered Christmas and in that spring-time garden. I know that life is as the artists show it, not as those men see it who use only the mind. They no longer know the real life or the speech of the artists—the speech of the cathedrals of Chartres and Strasbourg and Salisbury ; of the great symphonies and the ageless folk-songs ; of the Primavera and of the Sonnets. They have bartered Truth for Fact ; the divine sense of the child for the common sense of the adult ; the Reality for the Image.

It is forty years since I had my last sight of Geneva Street, but it and its little houses and gardens are, I believe, still there. That Christmas and that spring-time I know are still there. Nothing that settles into the human heart can ever die, though the heart itself die. That first Christmas and that first springtime, being felt so keenly, came to life, and somewhere they still live, a portion of some beautiful thing, of some immortal hour, some piercing passion. And when the hollow imitations of life press too closely upon me, I can always find them again—in a Kate Greenaway drawing, in the odour of a tangerine, in the sight of a crystallised fruit, in the perfume of a street-hawker's daffodils or violets. That Christmas was all Christmases, that springtime all springtimes ; Freda was all the friends I have known. They are all there, preserved for ever, not in the marble rigour of the past but in the pulse of one life's present. They can never . . .

But at that point the assistant of that gallery came forward to attend me. He had kept me waiting twenty-five seconds.